Jus.
FOCUS

Get Stuff Done, Concentrate on What Matters Most, and Unlock Your True Potential.

EMORY LOVE

© Copyright 2024 - All rights reserved.

The content inside this book may not be duplicated, reproduced, or transmitted without direct written permission from the author or publisher.

Under no circumstances will any blame or legal responsibility be held against the publisher, or author, for any damages, reparation, or monetary loss due to the information contained within this book, either directly or indirectly.

Legal Notice:

This book is copyright protected. It is only for personal use. You cannot amend, distribute, sell, use, quote or paraphrase any part, or the content within this book, without the consent of the author or publisher.

Disclaimer Notice:

Please note the information contained within this document is for educational and entertainment purposes only. All effort has been executed to present accurate, reliable, up to date, complete information. No warranties of any kind are declared or implied. Readers acknowledge that the author is not engaging in the rendering of legal, financial, medical, or professional advice. The content within this book has been derived from various sources. Please consult a licensed professional before attempting any techniques outlined in this book.

By reading this document, the reader agrees that under no circumstances is the author responsible for any losses, direct or indirect, that are incurred as a result of the use of the information contained within this document, including, but not limited to, errors, omissions, or inaccuracies.

TABLE OF CONTENT

INTRODUCTION
   How Do I Know?
   What This Book Is, and What It Is Not
   How to Read This Book

CHAPTER 1
Understanding Focus
   Types of Focus
   The Process of Focusing
   Why is Focus Important
   Costs of Lack of Focus
   Reduced Creativity
   Debunking the Myth of Multitasking
   Identifying Common Distractions in Modern Life
   How Focused Are You? Quiz

CHAPTER 2
Identifying Your Focus Triggers
   Personal Motivation
   Environmental Factors
   Mental and Emotional States

CHAPTER 3
Techniques To Enhance Focus
   Mindfulness and Meditation
   Time Management Strategies
   Cognitive Techniques

CHAPTER 4
Deep Work And Flow

CHAPTER 5
The Art Of Single Tasking

Attention Residue
Cognitive Bottlenecks
Chunking and Batching
The Pomodoro Technique
The 80/20 Rule (Pareto Principle)
Adopting a Single-Tasking Mindset

CHAPTER 6
Energy Management
Introduction to Energy Management
Understanding Energy Cycles
Identifying Peak Periods
Optimizing Your Energy
Recharging Rituals

CHAPTER 7
Creating Focus-Friendly Habits
CONCLUSION

INTRODUCTION

Have you ever sat in front of your computer, staring at a long to-do list, and you feel completely overwhelmed? Maybe you've had days where you can't focus no matter how hard you try, or you start one task and get distracted by many others. Trust me, I've been there.

One morning, I found myself drowning in a sea of unfinished tasks. My to-do list was a mile long, and I hadn't made a dent in it. The turning point came when I missed an important deadline because I got sucked into a social media rabbit hole. That's when I knew something had to change.

The good news? There's a way out of this cycle, and it starts with just one thing: focus. This book is about helping you find that focus, use it to get stuff done, and ultimately unlock your true potential. It's about cutting through the noise, identifying what's truly important, and making real progress towards your goals.

In This Book, I Am Going to Show You How to:

- Identify the biggest time-wasters and focus-zappers in your life (spoiler alert: social media is public enemy #1) and cut them out for good.
- Develop powerful habits to train your brain for laser-sharp concentration with simple daily exercises.
- Use psychological tricks to overcome procrastination and end "I'll do it later" for good.
- Set crystal-clear priorities to focus your energy on what matters most.
- Create a distraction-proof environment at home and work with easy feng shui tips.
- Manage your time in a way that works for your personality and life.

- Use simple tech tools and apps to boost your focus, without getting sucked into social media.
- Integrate productive habits and focus boosters into your daily routine so they stick.

And look, I'm not going to lie to you - none of this is easy. Developing intense focus and mental toughness takes work. But the strategies I'll share are realistic, backed by science and personal experience, and I'll break them down into simple steps you can actually follow.

By the end of this book, you'll go from feeling scattered and unproductive to a highly focused and productive individual. Just imagine what you could accomplish with a clear mind and limitless concentration!

How Do I Know?

You might be wondering how some random person (me) is qualified to teach you about concentration and productivity. That's a fair question.

The truth is, I used to be one of the most unfocused, all-over-the-place person you'd ever meet. My mind was always racing, and I constantly juggled a million tasks without really completing any of them, plus I easily let every little distraction derail me.

I'd start my day with a plan to power through my most important tasks, only to look up hours later and realize that I had gotten sucked into endless YouTube videos or re-edited the morning away. Again!

My lack of focus wasn't just zapping my productivity - it was stressing me out, tanking my self-esteem, and making me feel like a complete loser who couldn't get their life together.

I knew I had to make a change, but typical productivity advice wasn't cutting it. I'd try technique after technique, but nothing seemed to stick. Until one day, I finally lost a project worth thousands of dollars.

At that moment, I knew I had to approach my focus issues like a scientist. I studied the psychology of attention and motivation. I experimented relentlessly to find strategies that actually worked for me (and tossed out all the stuff that fell flat). Little by little, I optimized my habits and environment to enable incredible focus.

It wasn't easy as there were many slip-ups, procrastination bombs, and wasted days. Eventually, I became someone who could focus on important tasks for hours, tackle major projects effortlessly, and prioritize what truly deserves my energy.

These days, I have a thriving business, great personal relationships, and the mental clarity to pursue hobbies and passion projects. All because I mastered focus.

I'm not a superhuman or naturally focused person. I'm just a regular individual who overcame focus struggles, one step at a time. If I can do it, you can too.

What This Book Is, and What It Is Not

Let's get one thing straight - this isn't a vague, lecture-filled productivity book with useless fluff. There are no cheesy pep talks or unrealistic advice like "wake up at 4 AM to crush it!"

No, this book is a no-BS guide to developing intense focus with realistic, step-by-step strategies that anyone can follow. No gimmicks or miracle cures—just proven techniques that work.

Here's what you can expect:
- Straightforward advice and simple focus-boosting tactics, explained in clear language. No overwhelming research studies or jargon. This book prioritizes easy-to-follow steps over scholarly fluff.

- Concepts and strategies backed by scientific research and real-world examples. You'll find insights from neuroscience, psychology, and personal development, all designed to help you understand the why behind the how.
- Tons of personal stories and real-life examples illustrate the principles in action. I'll show you how I implement these focus strategies in my own life, including the struggles, failures, and mistakes.
- Plenty of hands-on exercises to try out the material as you go. You won't just read about concentration; you'll actively apply the techniques so they really click.
- Absolutely no judgment or assumptions about your current situation. Whether you struggle with social media addictions, chronic procrastination, or you bounce between tasks like a ping-pong ball, this book meets you where you are and helps chart a new course.

This book is not:

- It's not a magic solution that will turn you into a Zen master overachiever overnight. Developing intense focus takes hard work and commitment. This book provides a roadmap, but you still have to take the journey.
- It doesn't rehash the same tired advice you've heard a million times. This book offers fresh perspectives and unique focus-enhancing strategies you won't find elsewhere.
- Finally, it won't bore you with uninspired writing. My goal is to make this wildly readable and even entertaining—because who wants a dry, textbook-style snoozefest?

How to Read This Book

This book is meant to be a fun adventure, not a grueling slog. So I've purposefully structured it in a way that makes digesting and implementing the material as straightforward (and hopefully even enjoyable) as possible.

First off, each chapter covers one key focus-enhancing principle and breaks it down into bite-sized concepts and actionable steps. You can power through this book from cover to cover or jump around to the sections that feel most relevant to your life right now.

Every chapter also opens with a motivating quote that captures the theme. Some will make you think, others might even make you chuckle. Either way, these little nuggets of wisdom will provide you with an energizing jumpstart.

But this book isn't meant to be read passively. It's designed for active participation, reflection, and implementation. That's why every chapter includes:

- Thought-provoking questions to help you see how the concepts apply to your life and identify areas for growth. Don't just skim past these—pause and really think about them and answer them!
- "Focus Booster" actions you can try right away. These are the concrete tactics I'll explain in detail.
- "Now It's Your Turn" prompts you to put what you've learned into practice immediately. Working through these is crucial.
- "Pro Tip" boxes with bonus insights or advanced focus advice.

The goal is to make this an interactive experience where you engage in self-reflection and real work to improve your concentration skills.

To get the most out of this book, go through it chapter by chapter at first. Build a strong foundation by mastering the early focus tactics before moving on.

But feel free to bounce around as needed! If a particular chapter addresses your current needs or challenges, start there. You can always return to the other sections later.

Throughout the book, you'll get a behind-the-scenes look at how I apply these techniques in my daily life and how I tackle challenges. These stories are meant to provide clarity and relatability, not to brag. I'm an open book, flaws and all. You'll hear about my biggest failures, the distractions I've fallen for, and the realizations that helped me get back on track.

I hope that as I share my experiences, you'll see yourself reflected in them. Maybe you'll nod along thinking, "Yeah, I do that too!" or have an "Oh, that's why I get so distracted" moment.

I want you to walk away thinking, "If they can transform their focus, I can too."

Questions to Reflect On:

- Which area of your life is suffering most from lack of focus or concentration? Work, hobbies, relationships? Get clarity on your biggest pain points.
- How would your life be different if you could give 100% of your attention and energy to your top priorities?
- What are your biggest focus distractors and time wasters? Be brutally honest here!

Now It's Your Turn:

Grab a notebook or open a fresh doc on your computer. Write down 3 specific goals or areas of your life you want to apply intense focus towards.

For each one, jot down:

- Why this matters to you (your motivating "why")
- One or two current bad habits or distractions that pull your focus away

- What you hope to achieve or change by concentrating fully in this area

We'll revisit these goals throughout the book and adjust as you implement new focus-enhancing strategies.

So, if you're ready to cut through the noise and focus on what's most important...let's get started!

CHAPTER 1
Understanding Focus

You might have heard a lot about the word focus. I mean this book is about how to focus, so what exactly is a focus, and why is it so important in our lives?

I like to think of focus as a personal superpower, because it helps you zero in on what truly matters, whether it's a project at work, a hobby you love, or spending quality time with friends and family. When you focus, you can achieve more in less time and enjoy the process a lot more.

Focus is all about directing your attention to one thing at a time. Imagine you're holding a flashlight in a dark room. When you turn it on, the light shines on one spot, and it makes everything else fade into the background. That's what focus does for your mind. It helps you shine a light on what's important, so you can see it clearly and work on it effectively.

Now, why is focus so important? In the fast-paced world that we live in, distractions are everywhere. Your phone, social media, emails, and even your own thoughts can easily pull you away from what you're doing. Without good focus, it's easy to start a task, get distracted, and end up not finishing anything. Have you ever started cleaning your room, but then found an old photo album and got lost in the memories instead? That's a classic example of losing focus.

Good focus means you can stay on track and finish what you start. But focus isn't just about work. It also helps you enjoy your personal life more. If you love painting, being focused allows you to get lost in your art, and enjoy every brushstroke without your mind wandering. Or if you're spending time with loved ones, it helps you to be fully present. To really listen and engage, and make those moments more meaningful.

Let me share a story about my friend, Alex. Alex works as a freelance software developer and loves what he does. But a few months ago, he noticed he was struggling to keep up with his tasks. He would start working on a piece of code, but then an email notification would pop up, or a friend would call him to chat. And by the end of the day, he felt like he had worked hard but hadn't accomplished much.

Alex's struggle with focus left him feeling frustrated, and overwhelmed. He knew he was capable of more, he could take on more jobs but distractions were constantly getting in his way. He often felt like he was spinning his wheels without making any real progress.

In the coming chapters, I'll share how I helped Alex to overcome these challenges and dramatically improve his focus. You'll learn about the strategies he used and how you can apply them to your own life to boost your productivity and find more satisfaction in your work and personal activities.

The Science Focus

Now that we've got a basic understanding of what focus is, let's go a bit deeper into the science behind it. Don't worry; I'll keep it simple and relatable. By understanding how focus works in your brain, you'll be better equipped to harness it in your daily life.

How the Brain Focuses

Our brains are amazing, complex machines. They help us think, feel, and do the things we need to do each day. But when it comes to focus, there are some specific parts of the brain that play a key role.

Your brain is like a big city and in this city, there are many different neighborhoods, each with its own function. The part of the brain that's like the city's control center is called the prefrontal cortex. This is the area right behind your forehead. It's responsible for things like planning, decision-making, and, you guessed it, focusing.

When you decide to focus on something, like reading a book or working on a project, the prefrontal cortex lights up. It helps you block out distractions and concentrate on the task at hand. Think of it like a traffic cop, directing your attention to where it needs to go and blocking out the unnecessary stuff.

But the prefrontal cortex doesn't work alone. It gets help from other parts of the brain, like the parietal cortex, which processes sensory information, and the thalamus, which acts as a relay station for signals coming in and out of the brain. Together, these parts form a network that allows you to focus.

Let's put this into a story. Imagine you're in a library, trying to study for an important exam. There are people around you chatting, and typing on their laptops, and there's even someone playing music through their headphones a bit too loudly. Initially, it'll be hard to concentrate. But when you decide to really focus, your prefrontal cortex steps in, like a traffic cop, and starts to filter out the background noise. You stop noticing the chatter and the music, and you zero in on your textbook. That's your brain's focus network at work.

Another key player in this process is the reticular activating system (RAS). This is a cluster of nerves located at the brainstem that acts as a filter for all the information your brain processes. It decides what's important and what's not, and helps you focus on the task at hand. For example, if you're at a noisy party but someone says your name, you'll immediately tune in to that conversation. That's your RAS in action.

The Role of Neurotransmitters

There are chemical messengers in your brain that also help you focus. These are called neurotransmitters, and they play a crucial role in how well you can concentrate.

Two of the most important neurotransmitters for focus are dopamine and norepinephrine. They are what I like the brain's motivational speakers and energy boosters.

Dopamine is often called the "feel-good" neurotransmitter. It's released when you do something enjoyable, like eating your favorite food or finishing a task. It's like a little pat on the back from your brain, saying, "Good job! Keep going!" When you're working on something that interests you, dopamine helps you stay engaged and motivated.

Norepinephrine, on the other hand, is like your brain's adrenaline. It kicks in when you need to pay attention and stay alert. If you're in a situation that requires quick thinking, like driving in heavy traffic or playing a fast-paced game, norepinephrine helps you stay sharp and focused.

I want you to think of a time when you were really excited about a project or a hobby, maybe something creative like painting or building a model. You felt a sense of joy and satisfaction every time you made progress. That's dopamine at work. It kept you motivated and eager to continue.

Now, if you were preparing for a big presentation and you needed to stay alert, remember all your points, and respond to any questions from the audience. It is the norepinephrine that will help you stay on top of your game, and keep you focused and ready to react in these high-pressure situations.

But it's not just about having these neurotransmitters; it's also about having the right balance. Too little dopamine can make you feel unmotivated and distracted, while too much can make you overly excited and jittery. The same goes for norepinephrine – too little, and you might feel sluggish; too much, and you could feel anxious.

Maintaining this balance is crucial for good focus. And while it sounds complicated, your brain is pretty good at managing it, especially if you take care of your overall health. Eating well, getting adequate sleep, and regular exercise all help keep these neurotransmitters in check, and ready to support your brain's ability to focus.

Brain Waves and Focus

Another fascinating aspect of focus is the role of brain waves. Our brains are constantly producing electrical activity, which can be measured in waves. There are different types of brain waves, each associated with different states of mind.

- **Beta waves** are the fast, low-amplitude waves that dominate our brains when we're awake and alert. These are the waves of concentration and problem-solving.
- **Alpha waves** are slower and have a higher amplitude, and they appear when we're in a relaxed, yet alert state, such as during meditation or while daydreaming.
- **Theta waves** are even slower and are seen during light sleep or deep relaxation.
- **Delta waves** are the slowest type of brain waves and are predominant during deep sleep.

When you need to focus, your brain ramps up beta wave activity.

Types of Focus

There are two main types we'll look at: sustained focus and selective attention. Understanding these can help you recognize how your brain operates in various situations.

Sustained Focus

Sustained focus, also known as sustained attention, is the capacity to concentrate on a single task or activity for a prolonged period. This type of focus is crucial when you're working on tasks that require continuous effort, such as studying for an exam, writing a report, or even reading a book.

Think of sustained focus as running a marathon. It's not about speed but about maintaining a steady pace over a long distance. Just like a marathon runner needs endurance, your brain needs mental endurance to keep concentrating on a task without getting distracted.

Sarah is a writer who often works on long, complex novels. Writing a book is no small feat; it requires hours of sustained focus. Initially, Sarah found it challenging to stay focused for long periods. She would write for a bit, then open her emails, browse social media, or even do some household chores. It was frustrating for her because she knew she had the ideas and the skills but she still struggled to maintain the focus needed to complete her work.

Sustained focus is essential not just for work or study but for any activity that requires prolonged attention. Whether you're playing a musical instrument, practicing a sport, or even cooking a complicated recipe, being able to maintain your focus over time is the key to doing it well.

Another example of sustained focus is studying for an important exam. If you're a student preparing for your finals. You need to review your notes, read textbooks, and solve practice problems. All of this requires you to sit down and concentrate for a long time. Without sustained focus, you might find yourself skimming through pages without really absorbing the information, or getting up every few minutes to check your phone or grab a snack.

Sustained focus is like building muscle. The more you practice, the more robust it becomes. Athletes, artists, and professionals across all fields rely on their ability to maintain focus for long periods. It's what allows them to practice, perfect their skills, and achieve their goals.

Selective Attention

Selective attention is the capacity to concentrate on one specific thing while ignoring other irrelevant information. Think of it as having a spotlight in your mind that shines on what's important while everything else fades into the background.

Just like the example I gave earlier, if you're at a noisy party and someone says your name, you'll immediately tune in to that conversation. Despite the people talking, the music playing very loudly, and the movement around you, you will be able to focus on the conversation you're having with that person. This ability to tune out the background noise and concentrate on one thing is selective attention.

Selective attention is like having a mental filter. It helps you decide what to focus on and what to ignore. This is especially important in today's world, where we're constantly bombarded with information from various sources like social media, news, and our own thoughts.

Selective attention can also be seen in sports. Take a basketball player, for example. When they're on the court, they need to focus on the game – dribbling, passing, shooting, and defending. The crowd might be cheering loudly, the coach shouting instructions, and their opponents trying to distract them. Despite all this, the player stays focused on their actions and the game strategy. This ability to filter out the noise and concentrate on the task is crucial for their performance.

Both sustained focus and selective attention are vital for different aspects of life. Sustained focus helps you keep your attention on long-term tasks, while selective attention allows you to filter out distractions and focus on what's important at any given moment. Understanding these types of focus can help you recognize how to harness them effectively in various situations.

The Process of Focusing

Here's a step-by-step look at how focusing works in practice:

- **Goal Setting**: Your brain starts by setting a clear goal. This goal acts as a roadmap for your focus. For instance, if your goal is to finish a report, your prefrontal cortex identifies the steps needed to complete it.
- **Information Filtering**: The RAS filters out distractions. It decides which sensory inputs are important and which ones to ignore. If you're working on your report, the RAS helps you ignore the sounds of people talking nearby.
- **Sustaining Attention**: Your prefrontal cortex helps you maintain attention on your task. This involves continuously checking if you're still on track and readjusting your focus as needed. If you get distracted, this part of the brain pulls you back to the task.
- **Switching Focus**: Sometimes, you need to switch tasks. Cognitive flexibility allows your brain to shift attention from one task to another smoothly. This ability is crucial when managing multiple responsibilities.

Let's make this more relatable. Do you remember Sarah, the writer that I mentioned, was struggling earlier? Sarah decided she desperately needed to focus and finish her manuscript. Here's how she uses the process of focus:

- **Goal Setting**: Sarah started by setting a clear goal to write for two hours each day without distractions. This goal acted

as a roadmap for her focus. For instance, if her goal was to finish a chapter, her prefrontal cortex identified the steps needed to complete it.
- **Information Filtering**: To help her focus, Sarah created a dedicated writing space free from distractions. She put her phone on airplane mode and wore noise-canceling headphones. By controlling her environment, she helped her Reticular Activating System (RAS) filter out distractions. The RAS decided which sensory inputs were important and which ones to ignore. While working on her book, the RAS helped her ignore the sounds of people talking nearby or notifications from her phone.
- **Sustaining Attention**: As she started writing, Sarah's prefrontal cortex helped her maintain attention on her task. This involved continuously checking if she was still on track and readjusting her focus as needed. Whenever her mind started to wander, she took a deep breath and refocused on her work. She used a timer to write in 25-minute intervals with short breaks in between. This way, she could sustain her attention for longer periods.
- **Switching Focus**: Occasionally, Sarah needed to switch between different sections of her novel or different tasks, like editing or brainstorming. Her brain's cognitive flexibility allowed her to shift attention from one task to another smoothly. This ability was crucial for managing multiple aspects of her writing without losing her train of thought.

By following this process, Sarah was able to improve her focus significantly. She covered more material each day, her productivity increased, and she felt more satisfied with her work. Her ability to focus effectively made all the difference in her writing journey.

Why is Focus Important

Focus encompasses more than simply the ability to concentrate on a task; it's a fundamental skill that impacts every aspect of our lives. From our personal achievements to our professional success, focus plays a crucial role in how effectively we can manage and accomplish our goals. Here are some key reasons why focus is essential:

Achieving Goals

Setting and achieving goals requires a high level of focus. Whether it's finishing a work project, training for a marathon, or acquiring a new skill, the ability to concentrate on the necessary tasks is important. Focus helps you stay on track, avoid distractions, and maintain the discipline needed to reach your goals.

Enhances Productivity

When you can focus, you can work more efficiently. You're able to complete tasks faster and with better quality because your attention is fully on the task at hand. This leads to higher productivity and allows you to accomplish more in less time. For example, when Sarah, our writer friend, learned to focus better, she was able to write more pages each day and produce higher-quality work.

Improves The Quality of Work

Focused work leads to better outcomes. When you concentrate on a task, you can pay attention to details, think critically, and produce higher-quality work. This applies to all fields, from creative endeavors like writing and art to technical tasks like coding or data analysis.

Boosts Creativity

Creativity often requires deep, uninterrupted focus. When you're able to immerse yourself in a task without distractions, you can enter a state of flow where your best ideas and work emerge. Artists, writers, and innovators all benefit from the ability to focus deeply on their craft.

Reduces Stress

A focused mind is a calmer mind. When you're able to concentrate on one thing at a time, you feel more in control and less overwhelmed by the myriad of tasks and distractions. This reduces stress and anxiety and contributes to better mental health.

Strengthens Relationships

Focus is crucial in personal relationships too. Being present and attentive in conversations and shared activities shows others that you value and respect them. It fosters deeper connections and better communication.

Facilitates Learning and Growth

Learning new skills and acquiring knowledge requires sustained focus. Whether you're a student studying for exams or a professional keeping up with industry trends, the ability to concentrate enhances your ability to absorb and retain information.

Enhances Decision-Making

Good focus allows for better decision-making. When you're able to concentrate, you can weigh options more carefully, consider the consequences, and make more informed choices. This applies to both personal and professional decisions, that help you navigate life's challenges more effectively.

Costs of Lack of Focus

When we talk about focus, it's important to understand the flip side: i.e. what happens when we lack focus. The consequences can be both significant and far-reaching, and it can affect our productivity, relationships, and overall well-being.

Decreased Productivity

One of the most immediate and noticeable effects of a lack of focus is decreased productivity. When you can't concentrate on a task, it takes longer to complete, and the quality of your work may suffer. Imagine trying to write an important report for work. If you're constantly distracted by emails, social media, or office chatter, you'll find it hard to gather your thoughts and produce coherent, high-quality work.

The constant switching between tasks – known as task-switching – can result in a substantial decrease in productivity. Research has shown that it can take up to 25 minutes to regain full focus after a distraction. So, if you're frequently interrupted, you're likely losing a substantial amount of productive time each day.

Increased Stress and Anxiety

A lack of focus can also contribute to higher levels of stress and anxiety. When you're unable to complete tasks efficiently, you may feel overwhelmed by the growing list of things you need to do. This sense of being constantly behind can create a vicious cycle where stress further diminishes your ability to focus, leading to more stress.

Poor Quality of Work

When you can't focus, the quality of your work often suffers. This is because effective focus allows you to give your full attention to the details and nuances of a task, and it leads to better outcomes. In contrast, a lack of focus can result in mistakes, overlooked details, and a general decline in the standard of your work.

Strained Relationships

Focus isn't just important for work; it's crucial for personal relationships as well. When you're unable to focus during conversations or shared activities, it can make others feel undervalued and ignored. This lack of attention can strain relationships with your friends, family, and colleagues.

Missed Opportunities

Opportunities often come when we're paying attention. A lack of focus can result in missed opportunities because you aren't fully present or engaged. Whether it's an important networking event, a chance to learn a new skill, or simply being present to seize a moment of inspiration, being unfocused can mean missing out on important life and career opportunities.

Lowered Job Satisfaction

Job satisfaction is closely tied to how effective and productive we feel. When you're constantly battling distractions and struggling to focus, it can lead to a sense of dissatisfaction and burnout. Feeling like you're not performing at your best can diminish your enjoyment of your work and erode your overall job satisfaction.

Impact on Learning and Growth

Learning new skills or acquiring knowledge requires a high level of focus. Without it, absorbing new information and retaining it becomes challenging. This can obstruct your personal and professional development. If you're a student or a professional trying to keep up with industry developments, a lack of focus can put you at a disadvantage.

Reduced Creativity

Creativity often requires deep focus. When your mind is scattered, it's difficult to engage in the deep thinking and reflection that fuels creative ideas. Distractions can interrupt the flow of thoughts and disrupt the creative process.

Decline in Physical Health

Surprisingly, a lack of focus can also impact your physical health. Constantly shifting focus and dealing with distractions can be mentally exhausting, leading to physical symptoms like headaches, fatigue, and even weakened immunity over time. Stress from difficulty focusing can also lead to unhealthy habits, such as poor diet choices, insufficient exercise, and inadequate sleep.

Financial Costs

A lack of focus can have financial implications. Missed deadlines, poor quality work, and missed opportunities can all translate to loss of income or additional costs. For businesses, employees who struggle to focus may experience lower productivity and incur higher costs in terms of time and resources needed to correct mistakes or complete tasks.

For instance, a business that frequently misses project deadlines due to unfocused employees might face penalties or lose clients. This can have a direct impact on the company's bottom line. On a personal level, someone who can't focus might miss out on promotions or job opportunities, affecting their earning potential.

Debunking the Myth of Multitasking

Multitasking is frequently lauded as a beneficial skill because many people believe that juggling multiple tasks simultaneously can boost productivity and efficiency. However, research and real-life experiences suggest otherwise. The reality is that multitasking can hinder rather than help us achieve our goals.

At first glance, multitasking seems like a great way to get more done in less time. After all, if you can handle several tasks at once, you should be able to accomplish more, right? Unfortunately, this is an illusion. While you might feel busy, the quality and efficiency of your work often suffer when you divide your attention.

Let's use this simple example: talking on the phone while typing an email. On the surface, it seems like you're handling two tasks simultaneously. However, both tasks require cognitive resources, and your brain has to switch back and forth between them. This constant switching reduces your overall effectiveness and increases the likelihood of you making mistakes.

Cognitive Costs of Multitasking

When you multitask, your brain is not truly doing multiple things at once. Instead, it is rapidly switching between those tasks. This process, known as task-switching, comes with significant cognitive costs. Each time you switch tasks, your brain has to reorient itself, which consumes mental energy and time.

Research has shown that task-switching can reduce productivity by up to 40%. This decrease happens because the brain needs time to refocus and reestablish context with each switch. For example, if you're working on a report and then check your phone for a text message, it takes time for your brain to return to the same level of concentration on the report once you switch back.

Multitasking not only slows you down but also affects the quality of your work. When your attention is divided, it's harder to give each task the careful thought and attention it deserves. This can result in errors, oversights, and a general decline in the quality of your work.

Consider a chef preparing a complex meal. If the chef tries to simultaneously chop vegetables, monitor a simmering sauce, and prepare a dessert, the chances of making mistakes will increase. It may be that the chef will miss an ingredient, overcook the sauce, or poorly execute the dessert which can ruin the entire meal. Similarly, in any task that requires precision and creativity, multitasking can undermine your ability to perform at your best.

The Myth of Efficiency

Many people believe that multitasking saves time, but in reality, it often takes longer to complete tasks when multitasking. The time lost in switching between tasks adds up, and it makes the overall process less efficient. Studies have shown that people who multitask take longer to complete tasks and often end up redoing work due to errors they make while multitasking.

For instance, imagine trying to study for an exam while watching a TV show. You might think you're managing both tasks, but in reality, neither gets your full attention. You may find yourself zoning out on the TV show to reread a paragraph or missing key details in both the show and your study material. In the end, you might spend more time studying than if you had focused solely on your books first and then enjoyed the TV show as a reward.

Multitasking can also increase stress levels. When you try to manage multiple tasks at once, it can create a sense of chaos and overwhelm. The constant mental juggling can lead to feelings of anxiety and frustration, which further reduces your ability to concentrate and perform well.

Identifying Common Distractions in Modern Life

Let's face it: staying focused these days can be a real struggle. With technology constantly at our fingertips and the pace of life moving faster than ever, distractions are everywhere. Whether you're trying to work, study, or just get through your daily to-do list, something always seems to be pulling your attention away.

Digital Distractions

- **Social Media**

Social media platforms like Facebook, Instagram, X, and TikTok are among the biggest distractions in our modern life. These platforms are designed to capture and hold your attention with endless feeds of content, notifications, likes, and comments. It's easy to lose track of time while scrolling through updates, watching videos, or engaging in conversations.

- **Email and Messaging**

Whether it's work emails, personal messages, or group chats, the frequent pings and alerts can disrupt your concentration and divert you from your tasks. Each notification demands your attention and can lead to frequent task-switching, which reduces productivity.

- **Mobile Apps and Games**

Smartphones come loaded with various apps and games that can be highly addictive. From news apps to weather updates, and from simple puzzle games to complex strategy games, there's always something vying for your attention. The ease of access makes it tempting to take frequent breaks to check these apps.

- **Streaming Services**

Services like Netflix, YouTube, and Spotify offer endless entertainment options. It's tempting to watch a quick video or listen to music while working, but this can easily turn into hours of lost time. Autoplay features and personalized recommendations can keep you engaged longer than intended.

Environmental Distractions

- **Noise**

Noise is a common environmental distraction, and can include traffic noise, conversations, construction work, or any other background sounds. Noise makes it difficult to concentrate and can lead to frustration and stress.

- **Clutter**

A disorganized workspace can be a significant distraction. When your desk or work area is messy, it's harder to find what you need, and the visual clutter can overwhelm your senses, and make it difficult to focus on your tasks.

- **Interruptions from People**

Colleagues, family members, and friends can interrupt you with questions, conversations, or requests for help. These interruptions can break your concentration and make it challenging to get back into the flow of your work.

Mental Distractions

- **Stress and Worry**

Personal concerns, financial problems, health issues, and other stressors can occupy your mind, and make it hard to focus on your work. When your brain is preoccupied with worry, it's difficult to concentrate on the task at hand.

- **Daydreaming**

It's natural for your mind to wander from time to time, but frequent daydreaming can be a distraction. When you're constantly thinking about other things - be it future plans, past events, or random thoughts - it diminishes your ability to stay focused on your current task.

- **Boredom**

Tasks that are repetitive or not intellectually stimulating can cause boredom, which in turn leads to distraction. When you're not engaged with your work, you're more likely to seek out distractions to entertain yourself.

Technological Distractions

- **Push Notifications**

Push notifications from apps, including social media, news, and even some productivity apps, can be constant sources of distraction. Each notification demands immediate attention, and they pull you away from your work.

- **Internet Browsing**

The vast amount of information available on the internet can be a huge distraction. It's easy to get sidetracked by interesting articles, videos, and other content while you're supposed to be working on something else.

- **Online Shopping**

With the convenience of online shopping, it's easy to take a quick break to browse through products or make a purchase. However, this can quickly turn into an extended distraction as you compare products, read reviews, and get caught up in the process.

Sensory Distractions

- **Visual Clutter**

Bright screens, open tabs, and multiple windows on your computer can create visual clutter that distracts you. Each element on your screen can pull your attention away from the main task you're trying to focus on.

- **Temperature and Comfort**

Uncomfortable working conditions, such as a room that's too hot or too cold, or an uncomfortable chair, can be distracting. Physical discomfort can pull your focus away from your work as you try to adjust or find a more comfortable position.

Lifestyle Distractions

- **Poor Sleep**

Lack of adequate sleep can significantly impair your ability to focus. When you're tired, your brain struggles to concentrate, and you're more susceptible to distractions. Fatigue can make even minor distractions seem more disruptive.

- **Hunger and Thirst**

Being hungry or thirsty can be distracting because your body is signaling a need that must be addressed. This physical distraction will pull your attention away from your work as you think about food or drink.

- **Exercise and Physical Activity**

While exercise is generally good for focus and productivity, it can also be a distraction if you're thinking about fitting a workout into your schedule or feeling restless from sitting for too long without movement.

Task-Related Distractions

- **Overwhelming Workload**

An overwhelming number of tasks or a particularly challenging project can be distracting in itself. When you feel overwhelmed, it's harder to focus on one task because you're constantly thinking about everything else you need to do.

- **Lack of Clear Goals**

When you don't have clear goals or a clear understanding of what you need to accomplish, it's easy to get distracted. Clear goals offer guidance and help you maintain focus on what matters most.

How Focused Are You? Quiz

Answer the following questions to find out how focused you are. Choose the option that best describes your behavior or feelings. At the end, tally your points to see how you score!

1. **When working on a task, how often do you get distracted by your phone?**

(a) Almost never

(b) Occasionally

(c) Frequently

(d) Constantly

2. **How well do you set and follow clear goals for your tasks?**

(a) Very well, always set clear goals

(b) Mostly, but sometimes I forget

(c) Occasionally, but often vague

(d) Rarely set goals

3. **How do you handle background noise when trying to focus?**

(a) Easily ignore it

(b) It bothers me a little, but I manage

(c) Often distracted by it

(d) Always distracted and can't focus

4. **When you start a task, how long can you stay focused before needing a break?**

(a) More than an hour

(b) 30-60 minutes

(c) 15-30 minutes

(d) Less than 15 minutes

5. **How effectively can you switch between tasks without losing focus?**

(a) Very effectively

(b) Fairly well

(c) It takes me a while to adjust

(d) I struggle a lot

6. **Do you find yourself multitasking often?**

(a) Almost never

(b) Sometimes

(c) Frequently

(d) Constantly

7. **How organized is your workspace?**

(a) Very organized

(b) Somewhat organized

(c) Often cluttered

(d) Always cluttered

8. **How often do you complete tasks within the time you set for them?**

(a) Almost always

(b) Usually

(c) Sometimes

(d) Rarely

> 9. How do you feel after completing a focused work session?

(a) Accomplished and satisfied

(b) Mostly satisfied

(c) Somewhat tired

(d) Exhausted and unproductive

> 10. How well do you manage digital distractions (e.g., social media, emails)?

(a) Very well

(b) Fairly well

(c) Struggle sometimes

(d) Struggle a lot

Scoring

(a) = 4 points

(b) = 3 points

(c) = 2 points

(d) = 1 point

Add up your points to see how focused you are:

- **35-40:** Master! You have excellent focus and can manage distractions effectively.
- **25-34:** Pro! You're good at focusing but can still improve in some areas.

- **15-24:** Novice! You struggle with distractions but have the potential to improve.
- **Below 15:** Seeker! Focusing is a challenge for you, but with practice, you can get better.

Key Takeaways

1. Focus is a powerful tool that helps you zero in on what truly matters, enhancing both productivity and enjoyment in various activities.
2. Good focus is crucial for staying on track and completing tasks efficiently, especially in a world full of distractions.
3. The brain's prefrontal cortex plays a central role in directing attention and filtering out distractions, acting like a mental traffic cop.
4. Neurotransmitters like dopamine and norepinephrine are essential for maintaining motivation and alertness, supporting sustained focus.
5. Both sustained focus and selective attention are vital for different tasks, helping to maintain long-term concentration and filter out irrelevant information.

Reflective Questions

1. What are the key factors that help you maintain focus during important tasks?
2. How do you manage distractions in your environment to enhance your ability to concentrate?
3. In what ways can you balance your intrinsic and extrinsic motivations to stay engaged and committed to your goals?
4. How does your understanding of brain functions like the prefrontal cortex and neurotransmitters influence your approach to improving focus?
5. What strategies can you implement to strengthen both your sustained focus and selective attention in daily activities?

CHAPTER 2
Identifying Your Focus Triggers

Understanding focus is the first step, but knowing what specifically helps you focus can make all the difference in your productivity and satisfaction. In this chapter, we'll talk about identifying your focus triggers, starting with personal motivation.

Personal Motivation

Personal motivation is the driving force behind your actions. It's what propels you to start tasks, persevere through challenges, and achieve your goals. Understanding your motivation is crucial for enhancing your focus because it helps you stay engaged and committed to your tasks.

Motivation can be broadly classified into two types: intrinsic and extrinsic. Let's break these down and understand how they influence your ability to focus.

Intrinsic Motivation

Intrinsic motivation comes from within. It's the internal drive to do something because it's inherently interesting or enjoyable. When you're intrinsically motivated, you engage in an activity for the sheer pleasure and satisfaction it brings you, not for any external rewards.

Extrinsic Motivation

Extrinsic motivation, on the other hand, comes from external sources. It involves doing something to earn a reward or avoid a punishment. This type of motivation can be powerful but is often less sustainable than intrinsic motivation.

Balancing Intrinsic and Extrinsic Motivation

Both types of motivation are important and can work together to enhance your focus. Ideally, you want to find a balance where intrinsic motivation keeps you engaged and passionate about your tasks, while extrinsic motivation provides additional incentives and structure.

Exercise: Identifying Your Motivation

To understand your motivation better, try this exercise:

1. **List Your Activities:** Write down a list of activities you regularly engage in, both at work and in your personal life.
2. **Identify the Motivation:** For each activity, note whether your motivation is intrinsic, extrinsic, or a mix of both. Consider why you do each activity. Is it because you enjoy it, because you have to, or both?
3. **Reflect on Your Motivation:** Think about how your motivation affects your focus. Are you more focused on tasks you find intrinsically rewarding? Do extrinsic rewards help you stay on track for less enjoyable tasks?
4. **Enhance Your Motivation:** For activities that lack intrinsic motivation, try to find elements that you can enjoy or appreciate. For example, if you don't enjoy exercising but know it's important, try to find a form of exercise you like or set small, achievable goals to make it more rewarding.

Setting Personal Goals

Setting personal goals is an effective way to boost your focus. Clear, well-defined goals provide direction and purpose and help you stay motivated and concentrated on your tasks.

Goals give you something to aim for. They break down large tasks into manageable steps, making it easier to stay focused and monitor your progress... Having clear goals increases your likelihood of staying motivated and reduces the chances of getting distracted. Here's how you can set effective personal goals:

SMART Goals

One effective way to set goals is to use the SMART criteria. SMART stands for Specific, Measurable, Achievable, Relevant, and Time-bound. Let's break down each component:

- **Specific**: Your goal should be clear and specific. Instead of saying, "I want to get better at writing," say, "I want to write a 1,000-word article every week."
- **Measurable**: You should be able to track your progress. A measurable goal might be, "I want to increase my sales by 10% in the next quarter."
- **Achievable**: Your goal should be realistic and within reach. Setting an unachievable goal can be discouraging. For example, aiming to run a marathon next month if you've never run before is likely not achievable.
- **Relevant**: Your goal should be in alignment with your broader objectives and values. If your broader objective is career advancement, a relevant goal might be to complete a professional certification.
- **Time-bound**: Your goal should have a deadline. This helps create a sense of urgency and keeps you focused. For instance, "I want to finish my project by the end of this month."

Exercise: Setting SMART Goals

Let's practice setting SMART goals with an example related to improving focus.

1. **Identify an Area for Improvement:** Think about an area where you want to improve your focus. This could be a

specific task, project, or general aspect of your life, such as work, study, or a hobby.
2. **Define Your Goal:** Use the SMART criteria to define your goal. Here's an example:
- **Specific**: "I want to improve my focus during my study sessions."
- **Measurable**: "I will study for 2 hours each day without interruptions."
- **Achievable**: "I will start with 30-minute sessions and gradually increase to 2 hours over the next month."
- **Relevant**: "Improving my focus will help me perform better in my exams and achieve my academic goals."
- **Time-bound**: "I will achieve this by the end of the semester."
3. **Break Down the Goal**: Break your goal down into smaller, manageable steps. For example:
- Week 1: Study for 30 minutes without interruptions.
- Week 2: Increase to 1-hour study sessions.
- Week 3: Study for 1.5 hours without interruptions.
- Week 4: Reach the goal of 2-hour study sessions.
4. **Track Your Progress**: Maintain a journal or use an app to monitor your progress. Note any challenges you face and how you overcome them. Evaluate what is working well and what requires adjustment.
5. **Adjust as Needed**: Be flexible. If you find that your goal is too ambitious or not challenging enough, adjust it accordingly. The key is to keep moving forward and staying motivated.

Long-Term Goals vs. Short-Term Goals

When setting goals, it's important to distinguish between long-term and short-term goals. Long-term goals give you a big-picture vision, while short-term goals help you take actionable steps towards that vision.

For example, a long-term goal might be to write a novel. Short-term goals could include writing a chapter each month, developing a detailed outline, or setting aside a specific time each day for writing.

Exercise: Creating a Goal Hierarchy

To better understand how short-term goals can lead to long-term success, try creating a goal hierarchy:

1. **Identify Your Long-Term Goal**: Think about a major objective you want to achieve. Write it down at the top of your journal.
2. **Break It Down**: Below your long-term goal, write down several medium-term goals that will help you achieve it. For example, if your long-term goal is to write a novel, medium-term goals might include completing an outline, writing a certain number of chapters, and revising the manuscript.
3. **Detail Short-Term Goals**: Under each medium-term goal, write down specific short-term goals. These should be actionable steps you can take in the near future. For example, to complete an outline, your short-term goals might include brainstorming ideas, creating character profiles, and plotting the main events.
4. **Create a Timeline**: Assign deadlines to each goal, working backwards from your long-term goal. This will help you stay on track and see how each step leads to the next.
5. **Review Regularly**: Periodically review your goals to track your progress and make any necessary adjustments. Celebrate your achievements along the way to stay motivated.

Aligning Goals with Values

Another important aspect of setting personal goals is ensuring they align with your values. When your goals align with what genuinely matters to you, you're more likely to stay motivated and focused.

Take some time to reflect on your core values. What's most important to you in life? Is it family, career success, personal growth, creativity, or something else? Write down your top values and think about how your goals can support them.

For example, if one of your core values is health, set goals that prioritize your physical and mental well-being. This might include regular exercise, a balanced diet, and mindfulness practices. If creativity is a key value, set goals that allow you to express yourself, such as starting a new art project or learning a musical instrument.

Exercise: Values-Based Goal Setting

1. **Identify Your Values**: Write down your top 5-10 values. These could be anything from health and family to creativity and adventure.
2. **Reflect on Your Goals**: Look at your current goals and assess whether they align with your values. If not, think about how you can adjust them.
3. **Set New Goals**: Based on your values, set new goals that support what's most important to you. Ensure these goals are specific, measurable, achievable, relevant, and time-bound.
4. **Create an Action Plan**: Develop a step-by-step plan to achieve your new goals. Include short-term, medium-term, and long-term objectives.
5. **Monitor and Adjust**: Regularly review your goals and action plan. Make adjustments as needed to stay aligned with your values and maintain motivation.

Environmental Factors

Your environment is vital to your ability to concentrate. Creating a productive workspace and minimizing external distractions can significantly enhance your concentration and productivity.

A well-organized workspace can significantly enhance your ability to concentrate. Here are some key elements to consider when setting up your workspace.

Step 1: Choose the Right Location

The first step in creating a productive workspace is choosing the right location. Ideally, this should be a quiet area with minimal traffic and interruptions. If you work from home, consider setting up your workspace in a separate room or a quiet corner away from common areas.

Exercise: Evaluate Your Current Workspace

1. **Assess Noise Levels**: Take note of the noise levels in your current workspace. Is it quiet enough for you to concentrate, or are there frequent interruptions and background noise?
2. **Observe Traffic**: Notice the amount of foot traffic around your workspace. Are people constantly walking by and distracting you?
3. **Identify Distractions**: List any potential distractions in your current workspace, such as a TV, clutter, or an uncomfortable chair.
4. **Make a Plan**: Based on your assessment, make a plan to address any issues. This might involve moving to a quieter location, reorganizing your space, or adding elements to reduce noise.

Step 2: Optimize Lighting

Lighting plays a significant role in your ability to focus. Poor lighting can strain your eyes and make it difficult to concentrate, while good lighting can boost your energy and productivity.

Types of Lighting:

- **Natural Light**: If possible, set up your workspace near a window to take advantage of natural light. Natural light can improve your mood and reduce eye strain.
- **Task Lighting**: Use a desk lamp with adjustable brightness to provide focused light for specific tasks. Choose a lamp with a warm light to create a comfortable atmosphere.
- **Ambient Lighting**: Ensure your workspace is well-lit overall. Avoid harsh fluorescent lights and opt for soft, diffused lighting to reduce glare and create a pleasant environment.

Step 3: Ergonomic Setup

An ergonomic workspace is essential for maintaining comfort and focus over long periods. Poor ergonomics can lead to discomfort, fatigue, and even injury, all of which can detract you from your ability to concentrate.

Key Elements of Ergonomic Setup:

- **Chair**: Choose a chair with good lumbar support to maintain the natural curve of your spine. Adjust the height so that your feet are flat on the floor and your knees are at a 90-degree angle.
- **Desk**: Your desk should be at a height that allows your forearms to rest parallel to the floor when typing. Ensure there is enough space to keep your essentials within reach without cluttering your workspace.
- **Monitor**: Position your monitor at eye level to prevent neck strain. The top of the screen should be at or just below

eye level, and the monitor should be about an arm's length away.
- **Keyboard and Mouse**: Place your keyboard and mouse within easy reach, allowing your wrists to remain straight while typing and clicking. Consider using a wrist rest to reduce strain.

Step 4: Organize Your Workspace

A cluttered workspace can be a major distraction and can hinder your ability to focus. Organizing your workspace can help create a more efficient and pleasant environment.

Tips for Organizing Your Workspace:

- **Declutter**: Remove any unnecessary items from your desk and surrounding area. Keep only the essentials within reach.
- **Use Storage Solutions**: Invest in storage solutions such as shelves, drawers, and organizers to keep your workspace tidy. Label storage containers to easily find what you need.
- **Create Zones**: Designate specific areas for different tasks. For example, have a zone for computer work, a zone for reading, and a zone for taking notes.
- **Personalize**: Add personal touches to make your workspace more inviting. This could include plants, artwork, or motivational quotes.

Step 5: Maintain a Clean Workspace

Keeping your workspace clean is essential for maintaining focus. A clean environment reduces distractions and creates a more pleasant atmosphere.

Tips for Maintaining a Clean Workspace:

- **Daily Tidying**: Spend a few minutes at the end of each day tidying up your workspace. Put away items, wipe down surfaces, and organize your materials.

- **Weekly Cleaning**: Set aside time each week for a more thorough cleaning. Dust surfaces, vacuum or sweep the floor, and clean your equipment.
- **Regular Decluttering**: Periodically go through your items and remove anything you no longer need. This helps prevent clutter from building up over time.

Minimizing External Distractions

External distractions can disrupt your focus and hinder your productivity. Identifying and minimizing these distractions is crucial for maintaining concentration.

Step 1: Identify Common Distractions

The first step in minimizing distractions is to identify what typically disrupts your focus. Common distractions include noise, interruptions, and digital distractions.

Exercise: Identify Your Distractions

1. **Reflect on Your Day**: Think about a typical workday and note any distractions that commonly occur. This could include noise from outside, phone notifications, or interruptions from colleagues.
2. **Keep a Distraction Log**: For one week, keep a log of distractions you encounter. Note the time, type of distraction, and its impact on your focus.
3. **Analyze Your Log**: At the end of the week, review your log to identify patterns and common distractions. This will help you understand what disrupts your focus the most.

Step 2: Reduce Noise

Noise is one of the most common distractions in a workspace. Reducing noise can significantly improve your ability to focus.

Tips for Reducing Noise:

- **Noise-Canceling Headphones**: Invest in noise-canceling headphones to block out background noise. Listen to instrumental music or white noise to create a more focused environment.
- **Soundproofing**: If possible, add soundproofing elements to your workspace. This could include heavy curtains, rugs, or acoustic panels.
- **Quiet Hours**: If you share your workspace with others, establish quiet hours when everyone agrees to minimize noise. This could be a specific time of day when you can focus without interruptions.
- **Relocate**: If your current workspace is too noisy, consider relocating to a quieter area. This might involve moving to a different room or finding a quieter spot in a shared office.

Step 3: Manage Digital Distractions

Digital distractions, such as phone notifications, emails, and social media, can significantly disrupt your focus. Managing these distractions is essential for maintaining concentration.

Tips for Managing Digital Distractions:

- **Turn Off Notifications**: Disable non-essential notifications on your phone and computer. This includes social media, email, and app notifications.
- **Use Focus Mode**: Many devices have a focus or do not disturb mode that temporarily disables notifications. Use this feature during work or study sessions.
- **Set Specific Times for Checking Emails**: Instead of constantly checking your emails, set specific times during the day to read and respond to them. This helps you stay focused on your tasks without frequent interruptions.
- **Limit Social Media Use**: Use apps or browser extensions to limit your time on social media. Set specific times for social media use, such as during breaks or after work.

Step 4: Minimize Interruptions

Interruptions from colleagues, family members, or others can significantly disrupt your focus. Minimizing these interruptions is crucial for maintaining concentration.

Tips for Minimizing Interruptions:

- **Set Boundaries**: Communicate with those around you about your need for focused work time. Set clear boundaries and let them know when you're not to be disturbed.
- **Use Visual Cues**: Use visual cues, such as a closed door or a "do not disturb" sign, to signal that you're focusing and shouldn't be interrupted.
- **Schedule Interruptions**: If possible, schedule specific times for meetings, phone calls, or other interruptions. This helps you plan your work around these interruptions.
- **Create a Routine**: Establish a routine that includes focused work periods and times for interruptions. This helps you stay on track and manage interruptions more effectively.

Step 5: Create a Focus-Friendly Routine

A consistent routine can help you establish and maintain focus. By incorporating focused work periods and breaks into your routine, you can enhance your ability to concentrate and stay productive.

Tips for Creating a Focus-Friendly Routine:

- **Set Regular Work Hours**: Establish regular work hours and stick to them. This helps create a sense of structure and routine.
- **Plan Focused Work Periods**: Schedule specific periods for focused work. Use techniques like the Pomodoro Technique, where you work for a set period and then take a short break.

- **Incorporate Breaks**: Regular breaks are essential for maintaining focus. Schedule short breaks throughout your workday to rest and recharge.
- **Review and Adjust**: Regularly review your routine and make adjustments as needed. Pay attention to what works best for you and be flexible in making changes.

Mental and Emotional States

Stress, anxiety, and emotional turbulence can all disrupt your concentration and productivity. By understanding and addressing these internal factors, you can create a more conducive mental environment for concentration.

Stress Management

Stress is one of the most common barriers to focus. When you're stressed, your brain is in a state of heightened alertness, which can make it difficult to concentrate on tasks. Learning to manage stress effectively is crucial if you want to maintain focus and your overall well-being.

Step 1: Identify Sources of Stress

The first step in managing stress is to identify its sources. These can be external, like work pressures or personal responsibilities, or internal, like self-imposed expectations or negative thinking patterns.

Exercise: Identify Your Stressors

1. **Reflect on Your Day**: Think about your typical day and note any situations or activities that cause you stress. These might include work deadlines, family responsibilities, or social interactions.
2. **Keep a Stress Journal**: For one week, keep a journal where you record moments of stress. Note the time,

situation, and how you felt. This will help you identify patterns and common stressors.
3. **Analyze Your Journal**: At the end of the week, review your journal to identify the main sources of stress in your life. Look for patterns and recurring themes.

Step 2: Develop Healthy Coping Mechanisms

Once you've identified your stressors, it's important to develop healthy coping mechanisms to manage stress. These can include physical activities, relaxation techniques, and social support.

Tips for Developing Healthy Coping Mechanisms:

- **Exercise**: Physical activity is a powerful stress reliever. Regular exercise releases endorphins, which can improve your mood and reduce stress. Find an activity you enjoy, whether it's running, yoga, or dancing.
- **Relaxation Techniques**: Techniques like deep breathing, meditation, and progressive muscle relaxation can help calm your mind and reduce stress. Practice these regularly to build resilience against stress.
- **Social Support**: Connecting with friends and family can provide emotional support and reduce stress. Don't hesitate to reach out to your loved ones when you're feeling overwhelmed.
- **Hobbies and Interests**: Engaging in activities you enjoy can provide a mental break from stress and improve your overall well-being. Find time for hobbies and interests that bring you joy.

Step 3: Practice Mindfulness

Mindfulness is the practice of being fully present and engaged in the current moment. It can help you manage stress by promoting a sense of calm and awareness.

Tips for Practicing Mindfulness:

- **Mindful Breathing**: Take a few minutes each day to focus on your breath. Sit quietly, close your eyes, and take slow, deep breaths. Pay attention to the sensation of your breath entering and leaving your body.
- **Mindful Eating**: During meals, take the time to savor each bite. Notice the flavors, textures, and aromas of your food. Avoid distractions like TV or phones while eating.
- **Mindful Walking**: Go for a walk and pay attention to the sights, sounds, and sensations around you. Focus on each step and the feeling of the ground beneath your feet.
- **Body Scan**: Lie down or sit comfortably and focus on each part of your body, starting from your toes and moving up to your head. Notice any tension or discomfort and breathe into those areas.

Step 4: Set Boundaries

Setting boundaries is essential for managing stress. Boundaries help you protect your time and energy, reducing the likelihood of becoming overwhelmed.

Tips for Setting Boundaries:

- **Say No**: Don't be afraid to say no to commitments that don't align with your priorities or that you don't have the capacity to handle. It's important to protect your time and energy.
- **Limit Work Hours**: Set clear boundaries around your work hours. Avoid checking emails or working outside of your designated work time.
- **Communicate Needs**: Communicate your needs and boundaries to others. Let friends, family, and colleagues know when you're available and when you need time for yourself.
- **Create a Dedicated Workspace**: If you work from home, create a dedicated workspace that's separate from your

living areas. This helps establish a clear boundary between your work and personal life.

Emotional Regulation

Emotional regulation refers to the ability to manage and respond to your emotions in a healthy and productive way. Emotions like anger, frustration, and sadness can disrupt your focus if not properly managed. Learning to regulate your emotions is crucial for maintaining concentration and achieving your goals.

Step 1: Recognize and Acknowledge Your Emotions

The first step in emotional regulation is to recognize and acknowledge your emotions. Ignoring or suppressing emotions can lead to increased stress and decreased focus.

Exercise: Emotional Awareness

1. **Reflect on Your Emotions**: Take a few minutes each day to reflect on your emotions. Notice how you're feeling and identify any specific emotions you're experiencing.
2. **Label Your Emotions**: Use specific words to label your emotions. Instead of saying, "I feel bad," identify whether you're feeling sad, angry, frustrated, or anxious.
3. **Acknowledge Your Emotions**: Accept your emotions without judgment. Understand that it's okay to feel a range of emotions and that acknowledging them is the first step to managing them.

Step 2: Develop Healthy Emotional Outlets

Once you've acknowledged your emotions, it's important to develop healthy outlets for expressing and processing them. This can help prevent emotions from building up and interfering with your focus.

Tips for Developing Healthy Emotional Outlets:

- **Talk to Someone**: Sharing your feelings with a trusted friend or family member can provide emotional support and help you process your emotions.
- **Journaling**: Writing about your emotions in a journal can be a therapeutic way to express and understand your feelings. Set aside time each day to write about your experiences and emotions.
- **Creative Activities**: Engaging in creative activities like drawing, painting, or playing music can provide an outlet for expressing your emotions.
- **Physical Activity**: Physical activity can help release built-up tension and improve your mood. Find an activity you enjoy, whether it's running, dancing, or practicing yoga.

Step 3: Practice Self-Compassion

Self-compassion involves being kind and understanding toward yourself, especially during difficult times. It's an important aspect of emotional regulation and can help you manage your emotions more effectively.

Tips for Practicing Self-Compassion:

- **Be Kind to Yourself**: Treat yourself with the same kindness and understanding you would offer a friend. Avoid harsh self-criticism and negative self-talk.
- **Acknowledge Imperfections**: Understand that it's okay to make mistakes and have imperfections. Recognize that everyone has challenges and that it's a normal part of being human.
- **Practice Forgiveness**: Forgive yourself for past mistakes and let go of any lingering guilt or shame. Focus on learning and growing from your experiences.
- **Self-Compassionate Statements**: Use self-compassionate statements to support yourself during difficult times. For

example, say, "I'm doing the best I can, and it's okay to struggle sometimes."

Step 4: Manage Emotional Triggers

Emotional triggers are situations or events that evoke strong emotional reactions. Identifying and managing these triggers is crucial for maintaining focus and emotional balance.

Exercise: Identify and Manage Triggers

1. **Identify Triggers**: Reflect on situations or events that commonly trigger strong emotional reactions for you. Write them down.
2. **Understand the Impact**: Consider how these triggers affect your emotions and focus. Notice any patterns or recurring themes.
3. **Develop Coping Strategies**: Develop strategies for managing your emotional triggers. This might involve deep breathing, taking a break, or practicing mindfulness.
4. **Implement Strategies**: When you encounter an emotional trigger, implement your coping strategies to manage your reaction and maintain focus.

Step 5: Build Emotional Resilience

Emotional resilience is the ability to bounce back from adversity and maintain emotional balance. Building resilience can help you manage stress and emotions more effectively.

Tips for Building Emotional Resilience:

- **Develop a Positive Mindset**: Focus on the positive aspects of your life and cultivate a mindset of gratitude and optimism.
- **Learn from Challenges**: View challenges as opportunities for growth and learning. Reflect on what you can learn from difficult experiences.

- **Practice Adaptability**: Embrace change and be open to adapting to new situations. Flexibility can help you navigate challenges with greater ease.
- **Strengthen Relationships**: Build strong, supportive relationships with friends and family. Social support is a key factor in emotional resilience.

Key Takeaways

1. Understanding personal motivation, both intrinsic and extrinsic, is crucial for enhancing your focus and staying engaged with tasks.
2. Setting clear, well-defined goals using the SMART criteria provides direction and helps maintain motivation and concentration.
3. Creating a productive environment, including an ergonomic workspace and minimizing external distractions, significantly boosts focus and productivity.
4. Managing stress through healthy coping mechanisms, mindfulness, and setting boundaries is essential for maintaining focus and overall well-being.
5. Emotional regulation and self-compassion are key to managing emotions effectively, which in turn helps maintain concentration and achieve goals.

Reflective Questions

1. What types of activities do you find most intrinsically motivating, and how can you incorporate more of them into your daily routine?
2. How do your current goals align with your core values, and what steps can you take to ensure they support what matters most to you?
3. What changes can you make to your workspace to reduce distractions and enhance your ability to focus?

4. How do you currently manage stress, and what new strategies could you try to improve your focus and well-being?
5. In what ways can you practice self-compassion to better manage your emotions and maintain concentration on your tasks?

CHAPTER 3
Techniques To Enhance Focus

Enhancing your focus involves more than just setting goals and managing your environment. It requires adopting specific techniques that train your mind to concentrate better and longer. In this chapter, we'll explore various techniques to enhance your focus

Mindfulness and Meditation

Mindfulness and meditation are powerful practices that can significantly improve your focus and overall well-being. By training your mind to stay present, you can enhance your ability to concentrate on tasks and reduce the impact of distractions.

Benefits of Mindfulness

Mindfulness involves being fully present and engaged in the current moment, without judgment. Practicing mindfulness can bring numerous benefits that directly impact your ability to focus.

- **Reduced Stress**: Mindfulness helps lower your stress levels by promoting relaxation and reducing the impact of stressors. When you're less stressed, you're better able to concentrate on tasks.
- **Improved Attention**: Mindfulness trains your brain to stay focused on the present moment. This can enhance your attention span and reduce mind-wandering.
- **Better Emotional Regulation**: Mindfulness helps you become more aware of your emotions and manage them effectively. This can prevent emotional distractions and improve your overall focus.

- **Enhanced Cognitive Function**: Regular mindfulness practice has been shown to improve cognitive functions such as memory, problem-solving, and decision-making.

Exercise: Mindfulness Awareness

1. **Choose an Activity**: Select a daily activity, such as eating, walking, or brushing your teeth, to practice mindfulness.
2. **Focus on the Present**: During the activity, focus fully on the present moment. Notice the sensations, sounds, and feelings associated with the activity.
3. **Observe Without Judgment**: Observe your thoughts and feelings without judgment. If your mind wanders, gently bring your attention back to the activity.
4. **Reflect on the Experience**: After the activity, take a moment to reflect on your experience. Notice any changes in your stress levels or attention.

Daily Meditation Practices

Meditation is a specific practice within mindfulness that involves training your mind to focus and achieve a state of calm and clarity. Incorporating meditation into your daily routine can greatly enhance your focus.

Types of Meditation:

- **Focused Attention Meditation**: Involves focusing on a single point of reference, such as your breath, a mantra, or an object.
- **Body Scan Meditation**: Involves focusing on different parts of your body, noticing any sensations or tension.
- **Loving-Kindness Meditation**: Involves sending feelings of love and compassion to yourself and others.

Exercise: Basic Meditation Practice

1. **Find a Quiet Space**: Choose a quiet space where you won't be disturbed. Sit comfortably with your back straight and your hands resting in your lap.
2. **Focus on Your Breath**: Close your eyes and take a few deep breaths. Then, settle into a natural breathing rhythm. Focus on the sensation of your breath entering and leaving your body.
3. **Observe Your Thoughts**: As you meditate, thoughts will arise. Instead of engaging with them, simply observe them and let them pass. Then gently bring your focus back to your breath.
4. **Set a Timer**: Start with a short meditation session, such as 5-10 minutes. Gradually increase the duration as you become more comfortable with the practice.
5. **Reflect on Your Practice**: After your session, take a moment to reflect on your experience. Notice any changes in your focus, mood, or stress levels.

Exercise: Body Scan Meditation

1. **Lie Down or Sit Comfortably**: Find a comfortable position, either lying down or sitting. Close your eyes and take a few deep breaths.
2. **Focus on Your Body**: Start by focusing on your toes. Notice any sensations, tension, or relaxation.
3. **Move Up Your Body**: Gradually move your focus up your body, from your feet to your head. Spend a few moments on each body part, noticing any sensations.
4. **Breathe into Tension**: If you notice any areas of tension, imagine breathing into those areas. With each breath, feel the tension release.

5. **Reflect on Your Practice**: After the body scan, take a moment to reflect on your experience. Notice any changes in your relaxation or focus.

Exercise: Loving-Kindness Meditation
1. **Find a Quiet Space**: Choose a quiet space where you won't be disturbed. Sit comfortably with your back straight and your hands resting in your lap.
2. **Focus on Your Breath**: Close your eyes and take a few deep breaths. Settle into a natural breathing rhythm.
3. **Send Love to Yourself**: Silently repeat phrases such as "May I be happy. May I be healthy. May I be safe. May I be at ease."
4. **Send Love to Others**: Gradually extend these feelings to others, starting with loved ones, then acquaintances, and finally all living beings.
5. **Reflect on Your Practice**: After your session, take a moment to reflect on your experience. Notice any changes in your mood or focus.

Time Management Strategies

Effective time management is crucial for maintaining focus and productivity. By organizing your time efficiently, you can reduce stress and ensure that you're dedicating sufficient attention to your tasks.

The Pomodoro Technique

The Pomodoro Technique is a time management method that involves working in short, focused intervals with breaks in between. This technique can help you maintain concentration and avoid burnout.

Time Blocking

Time blocking is a time management technique that involves dividing your day into blocks of time dedicated to specific tasks. This method helps ensure that you're allocating enough time for each task and reduces the likelihood of multitasking.

Steps for Time Blocking:

1. **Identify Your Tasks**: Make a list of all the tasks you need to complete.
2. **Allocate Time Blocks**: Divide your day into blocks of time and allocate each block to a specific task. Be realistic about how long each task will take.
3. **Schedule Breaks**: Include regular breaks in your schedule to rest and recharge.
4. **Stick to the Schedule**: Follow your time blocks as closely as possible. Avoid switching tasks during a block.
5. **Review and Adjust**: At the end of the day, review your schedule and make any necessary adjustments for the following day.

Advanced Time Blocking

Once you're comfortable with basic time blocking, you can implement more advanced techniques to further enhance your productivity:

- **Theme Days**: Dedicate entire days to specific themes or types of work. For example, you might have a "Meeting Monday" where you schedule all your meetings, and a "Focus Friday" where you dedicate time to deep work.
- **Batching Similar Tasks**: Group similar tasks together and complete them in one block of time. This reduces the cognitive load of switching between different types of tasks.

- **Flexible Time Blocks**: While it's important to stick to your schedule, allow for some flexibility. If a task takes longer than expected, adjust your schedule accordingly.

Exercise: Advanced Time Blocking

1. **Choose a Theme**: Select a theme for each day of the week based on your work requirements.
2. **Batch Similar Tasks**: Identify similar tasks and group them into a single time block.
3. **Create a Flexible Schedule**: Allow for some flexibility in your schedule to accommodate tasks that take longer than expected.
4. **Evaluate and Adjust**: At the end of each week, evaluate the effectiveness of your time blocks and make any necessary adjustments for the following week.

Cognitive Techniques

Cognitive techniques involve training your mind to enhance focus and productivity. These techniques can help you develop a more positive mindset, visualize success, and stay motivated.

Visualization

Visualization is a cognitive technique that involves creating vivid mental images of your goals and the steps needed to achieve them. This technique can help you stay motivated, focused, and aligned with your objectives.

Steps for Visualization:

1. **Set Clear Goals**: Define clear, specific goals that you want to achieve.
2. **Create a Mental Image**: Close your eyes and create a detailed mental image of yourself achieving your goal.

Visualize the steps you need to take, the obstacles you might face, and how you'll overcome them.
3. **Engage Your Senses**: Make your visualization as vivid as possible by engaging all your senses. Imagine the sights, sounds, smells, and feelings associated with achieving your goal.
4. **Practice Regularly**: Practice visualization regularly, ideally daily. The more you practice, the more effective it will be.

Advanced Visualization

For more advanced visualization, incorporate these techniques:

- **Future Self Visualization**: Visualize yourself in the future after achieving your goals. Imagine how your life has changed and how you feel about your accomplishments.
- **Process Visualization**: Focus on visualizing the process rather than just the outcome. Imagine yourself working through each step of the process, overcoming obstacles, and staying motivated.
- **Affirmation Visualization**: Combine visualization with positive affirmations. As you visualize, repeat affirmations that reinforce your goals and self-belief.

Positive Affirmations

Positive affirmations are statements that you repeat to yourself to reinforce positive beliefs and attitudes. Using affirmations can help boost your confidence, motivation, and focus.

Steps for Creating Positive Affirmations:

1. **Identify Your Goals**: Think about the goals you want to achieve and the qualities you need to develop to reach them.

2. **Create Affirmations**: Write down positive affirmations that align with your goals and qualities. Use present tense and positive language.
3. **Repeat Daily**: Repeat your affirmations daily, ideally in the morning and before bed. Say them out loud or silently to yourself.
4. **Believe in Your Affirmations**: As you repeat your affirmations, believe in their truth and power. Visualize yourself embodying the qualities and achieving your goals.

Advanced Affirmation Techniques

To enhance the effectiveness of your affirmations, incorporate these advanced techniques:

- **Mirror Work**: Stand in front of a mirror and repeat your affirmations while looking into your eyes. This can help strengthen the connection between your words and your self-belief.
- **Affirmation Journaling**: Keep a journal where you write down your affirmations daily. Reflect on how they make you feel and any changes you notice in your mindset and behavior.
- **Combining with Visualization**: Combine your affirmations with visualization. As you repeat your affirmations, visualize yourself achieving your goals and embodying the qualities you desire.

Key Takeaways

1. Mindfulness and meditation can significantly enhance your ability to focus by reducing stress and improving cognitive functions.
2. The Pomodoro Technique helps maintain concentration and prevent burnout by working in short, focused intervals with breaks in between.

3. Time blocking involves organizing your day into dedicated time blocks for specific tasks, reducing the likelihood of multitasking and increasing productivity.
4. Visualization and positive affirmations are powerful cognitive techniques that can help you stay motivated and aligned with your goals.
5. Advanced time management strategies like theme days and batching similar tasks can further enhance your productivity and focus.

Reflective Questions

1. How can incorporating mindfulness and meditation into your daily routine improve your ability to concentrate on tasks?
2. In what ways can the Pomodoro Technique help you manage your workload and reduce burnout?
3. How can time blocking help you organize your day more effectively and reduce distractions?
4. What specific goals would benefit from regular visualization and positive affirmations, and how can you incorporate these techniques into your daily routine?
5. How can advanced time management strategies like theme days and batching similar tasks enhance your productivity and focus in your personal and professional life?

CHAPTER 4
Deep Work And Flow

Deep work is a concept popularized by Cal Newport, and it involves engaging in professional activities that require full concentration and push your cognitive capabilities to their limit. Deep work is more than just working hard; it's about working smart by immersing yourself fully in tasks that create the most value. To understand deep work, it's essential to differentiate it from shallow work.

Deep work is defined as activities performed in a state of distraction-free concentration that pushes your cognitive capabilities to their limit. These efforts create new value, improve your skills, and are hard to replicate. In contrast, shallow work consists of non-cognitively demanding tasks that are often performed while distracted and do not create much new value.

Differences between Deep Work and Shallow Work

To truly appreciate the power of deep work, it's important to understand how it differs from shallow work:

Deep Work:

- **Requires Full Attention**: Deep work demands undivided attention and full cognitive engagement. Think of it as a mental workout where your brain is fully engaged in solving complex problems or creating new ideas.
- **Creates High Value**: The output of deep work is significant and valuable. This might include writing a comprehensive report, designing a new product, or solving a challenging problem.

- **Improves Skills**: Engaging in deep work consistently helps you improve your skills and advance in your career. It's like lifting heavy weights at the gym; it makes you stronger over time.
- **Difficult to Replicate**: Because deep work is highly individualized and skill-intensive, it's hard for others to replicate your efforts. This uniqueness adds to its value.

Shallow Work:

- **Requires Minimal Attention**: Shallow work tasks can be performed while distracted and do not require much cognitive effort. Examples include answering emails, scheduling meetings, and other routine tasks.
- **Creates Low Value**: The output of shallow work is often repetitive and does not add significant value. These tasks are necessary but do not drive meaningful progress.
- **Does Not Improve Skills**: Since shallow work is not challenging, it does not contribute to skill development. It's like doing the same light exercise every day; it maintains your current level but doesn't help you improve.
- **Easy to Replicate**: Shallow work tasks are often straightforward and can be easily replicated or delegated to others.

Exercise: Identify Deep and Shallow Work

To help you distinguish between deep and shallow work in your own life, try this exercise:

1. **List Your Tasks**: Write down all the tasks you perform in a typical week.
2. **Categorize Tasks**: Divide them into two categories: deep work and shallow work. Be honest about the cognitive effort and value each task requires.

3. **Prioritize Deep Work**: Highlight the deep work tasks that are most important for your long-term goals. These are the tasks you should focus on to create significant value.
4. **Schedule Time**: Allocate dedicated time blocks in your calendar for deep work tasks. Ensure these periods are free from interruptions and distractions.

Benefits of Deep Work

Engaging in deep work offers numerous benefits, particularly in terms of productivity and creativity.

1. **Enhanced Focus:**
   - Deep work allows you to focus intensely on a single task, leading to higher-quality output.
   - It minimizes the time spent on context switching, which can drain mental energy. When you're fully immersed in a task, you can achieve a state of flow, where everything else fades away and you're at your most productive.
2. **Skill Improvement:**
   - By pushing your cognitive boundaries, deep work helps you develop and refine valuable skills. This continuous practice of deep work activities leads to mastery. Think of a musician practicing their instrument; the more they practice deeply, the better they become.
3. **Greater Efficiency:**
   - Deep work enables you to accomplish more in less time. The concentrated effort reduces the overall time required to complete complex tasks. You become more efficient because you're not wasting time on distractions or shallow work.
4. **Increased Satisfaction:**
   - Completing challenging tasks through deep work provides a sense of accomplishment and fulfillment. It can lead to a more meaningful and enjoyable work experience. There's a

profound satisfaction in knowing you've given your best effort and achieved something significant.

Case Study: Alex the Freelance Software Developer

Do you remember my friend Alex, the Freelance Software Developer? After we spoke, and I discussed a few strategies with him, Alex decided to embrace the concept of deep work. He began by identifying the tasks that required his full concentration and had the most significant impact on his goals, such as coding new features and solving complex bugs.

To create an environment conducive to deep work, Alex made several changes. He started by scheduling dedicated deep work sessions in the mornings, when he was most alert and free from interruptions. He also turned off notifications on his phone and computer, used noise-canceling headphones, and set clear boundaries with his friends and family, letting them know his work hours were sacred.

Alex developed a pre-work ritual to signal the start of his deep work sessions. Before starting his tasks, he would clear his desk, review his goals for the session, and spend a few minutes meditating to calm his mind and enhance his focus.

As he practiced deep work consistently, Alex noticed significant improvements in his productivity and the quality of his work. He completed projects faster and felt more satisfied with his achievements. By reducing distractions and fully engaging in his tasks, Alex was able to make meaningful progress and take on more challenging projects.

Exercise: Deep Work Planning

To get started with deep work, try this exercise:

1. **Identify Deep Work Tasks**: List the tasks that require deep work in your role. Consider the activities that demand

your full attention and have the most significant impact on your goals.
2. **Create a Schedule**: Allocate specific time blocks for deep work each day or week. Choose times when you're most alert and free from interruptions.
3. **Minimize Distractions**: Identify potential distractions and take steps to eliminate them during deep work sessions. This might include turning off notifications, using noise-canceling headphones, or finding a quiet workspace.
4. **Track Progress**: Monitor your progress and adjust your schedule as needed to optimize your deep work periods. Keep a journal to reflect on what works and what doesn't.

Creating Deep Work Habits

Developing consistent habits is essential for integrating deep work into your routine. By establishing rituals and routines, you can create a structured environment that supports sustained concentration and productivity.

Rituals and Routines

Establishing rituals and routines can help you transition into a deep work state more easily and maintain focus over extended periods.

Importance of Establishing Consistent Routines

- **Reduces Decision** Fatigue: Having a set routine minimizes the number of decisions you need to make each day, conserving mental energy for important tasks. When you know exactly what you need to do and when you can dive into work without hesitation.
- **Signals Transition**: Rituals signal to your brain that it's time to shift into deep work mode, making it easier to concentrate. This mental shift is crucial for maintaining focus and avoiding distractions.

- **Builds Momentum**: Consistent routines create a sense of momentum, making it easier to maintain productivity over time. When you establish a habit of deep work, it becomes second nature to engage in focused activities.

Examples of Effective Deep Work Rituals

- **Morning Routine**: Start your day with a consistent routine that includes activities like exercise, meditation, and a healthy breakfast. This sets a positive tone for the day and prepares your mind for deep work. For example, you might begin with a 10-minute meditation, followed by a 30-minute workout, and a nutritious breakfast.
- **Pre-Work Ritual**: Develop a pre-work ritual that signals the start of your deep work session. This could include clearing your desk, turning off notifications, and taking a few deep breaths. Such rituals help create a mental shift into focused work mode.
- **Time Blocking**: Schedule dedicated time blocks for deep work in your calendar. Treat these appointments with the same importance as meetings or other commitments. For instance, you might block off 9-11 AM for deep work, ensuring no interruptions during this period.
- **Midday Reset**: Incorporate a midday ritual to refresh your mind and body. This could be a short walk, a meditation session, or a healthy snack. Taking breaks helps prevent burnout and maintains your energy levels.
- **Evening Wind-Down**: End your day with a consistent evening routine that helps you relax and unwind. This prepares you for restful sleep and sets you up for a productive next day. An evening wind-down might include journaling about your day, reading a book, or practicing a few minutes of mindfulness.

Exercise: Create Your Deep Work Rituals

1. **Identify Key Rituals**: Choose rituals that resonate with you and support your deep work efforts. Consider your preferences and what activities help you transition into a focused state.
2. **Develop a Routine**: Write down a detailed routine for each ritual, including specific actions and timings. Ensure these rituals are realistic and achievable.
3. **Implement and Adjust**: Start implementing your rituals and adjust them as needed based on your experience. Be flexible and open to making changes to optimize your routine.
4. **Track Consistency**: Keep track of your rituals and routines to ensure consistency. Reflect on their impact on your productivity and focus.

Exercise: Daily Deep Work Journal

1. **Morning Reflection**: Each morning, take a few minutes to write down your goals for the day and any rituals you plan to follow. This helps set your intentions and prepares your mind for focused work.
2. **Evening Reflection**: At the end of the day, reflect on your deep work sessions. Note what worked well and any challenges you faced. This reflection helps you understand your progress and identify areas for improvement.
3. **Weekly Review**: At the end of each week, review your journal entries. Identify patterns and make adjustments to your routines as needed. This review helps you stay on track and continuously improve your deep work habits.

Advanced Deep Work Techniques

Once you've established basic deep work habits, you can implement advanced techniques to further enhance your productivity:

- **Monastic Approach**: Eliminate or drastically reduce shallow work and distractions. This approach involves dedicating entire days or weeks to deep work. For example, you might take a "deep work retreat" where you focus solely on a significant project without any interruptions.
- **Bimodal Approach**: Alternate between periods of deep work and periods of shallow work. For example, you might dedicate the mornings to deep work and the afternoons to administrative tasks. This balance helps you maintain focus and manage necessary but less demanding tasks.
- **Rhythmic Approach**: Establish a consistent daily rhythm for deep work. For instance, you might set aside the first two hours of each day for deep work. This rhythm helps create a habit of focused work.
- **Journalistic Approach**: Fit deep work sessions into your schedule whenever possible, similar to how journalists write articles on tight deadlines. This approach requires flexibility and the ability to switch into deep work mode quickly.

Exercise: Experiment with Advanced Techniques

1. **Choose a Technique**: Select an advanced deep work technique to experiment with based on your preferences and schedule. Consider which approach aligns best with your work style and commitments.
2. **Implement and Monitor**: Implement the technique for a specified period and monitor your progress. Keep a journal to track your experiences and reflect on the effectiveness of the technique.

3. **Reflect and Adjust**: Reflect on the effectiveness of the technique and make adjustments as needed. Try different approaches to find what works best for you.

Key Takeaways

1. Deep work requires undivided attention and leads to significant, valuable outcomes.
2. Shallow work is low-value, easily replicated, and does not improve skills.
3. Engaging in deep work enhances focus, improves skills, and increases efficiency.
4. Developing rituals and routines helps transition into a deep work state and maintain focus.
5. Advanced deep work techniques, like the Monastic or Bimodal approaches, can further enhance productivity.

Reflective Questions

1. How can you differentiate between your deep work and shallow work tasks?
2. What changes can you make to your environment to minimize distractions and support deep work?
3. How can establishing a pre-work ritual help you transition into a deep work state?
4. Which advanced deep work technique do you think would best suit your work style, and why?
5. How can regularly reflecting on your deep work sessions help you improve your focus and productivity?

CHAPTER 5
The Art Of Single Tasking

From responding to emails during meetings to catching up on work while watching TV, multitasking seems like a necessary strategy to keep up with our demanding lives. However, research and experience show that this approach can actually hinder your productivity and increase your stress levels. In this chapter, I am going to take you around the world of single-tasking, where the focus is on completing one task at a time with undivided attention.

Single-tasking is the practice of dedicating yourself to a single task until it is completed before moving on to the next. This approach leverages your brain's natural ability to concentrate deeply, leading to higher-quality work and greater efficiency. In this chapter, we'll explore why single-tasking is not just an old-fashioned notion but a powerful strategy for modern productivity.

Let's start by understanding two critical concepts that highlight the benefits of single-tasking: attention residue and cognitive bottlenecks. These concepts explain why our brains struggle with multitasking and how we can improve our focus by embracing a single-tasking mindset.

Embracing Single-Tasking

Transitioning from a multitasking mindset to a single-tasking approach requires a shift in how we view productivity. Instead of measuring success by the number of tasks we handle simultaneously, we should focus on the quality and completeness of our work. Single-tasking encourages deeper engagement, better problem-solving, and higher satisfaction with the tasks we undertake.

Throughout this chapter, we will explore the science behind attention residue and cognitive bottlenecks, providing practical strategies and exercises to help you adopt single-tasking in your daily life. You will learn how to identify and manage distractions, prioritize tasks effectively, and create an environment conducive to focused work.

By the end of this chapter, you will have a clear understanding of why single-tasking is a superior approach to managing your workload. You will be equipped with the tools and techniques needed to break free from the multitasking trap and harness the full power of focused, undivided attention.

Attention Residue

Attention residue is a fascinating yet frustrating phenomenon that plays a significant role in our ability to focus and perform tasks effectively. When we switch from one task to another, our brain doesn't just move seamlessly from the first task to the next. Instead, part of our attention remains stuck on the previous task, causing what is known as attention residue. This residual focus can disrupt our concentration and impair our performance on the new task.

To understand attention residue, let's imagine your brain as a computer with multiple programs running. When you switch from one program to another, the first program doesn't completely close; it continues to run in the background, consuming resources and slowing down the system. Similarly, when you switch from one task to another, your brain retains some focus on the previous task, which can interfere with your ability to concentrate fully on the new task.

This leftover attention doesn't just vanish immediately. It lingers, making it harder to fully engage with the new task. The more frequently you switch tasks, the more attention residue builds up, leading to decreased performance, increased errors, and higher levels of stress.

The Impact of Attention Residue on Productivity

Attention residue can significantly impair productivity. Each time you switch tasks, your brain needs time to adjust and refocus. This transition period, although it might seem brief, can add up over the course of a day, resulting in substantial time lost.

Research conducted by Dr. Sophie Leroy, a prominent researcher in the field of organizational behavior, provides compelling evidence of the impact of attention residue. In her studies, Dr. Leroy found that people who frequently switch tasks are less productive and more prone to mistakes than those who focus on one task at a time. Her research revealed that it takes an average of 23 minutes and 15 seconds to regain full concentration after being interrupted. This means that each time you switch tasks, you're potentially losing nearly half an hour of productive time.

Strategies to Minimize Attention Residue

Minimizing attention residue involves adopting practices that help you maintain focus and reduce task switching. Here are some effective strategies:

- **Batch Similar Tasks**

One of the most effective ways to minimize attention residue is to batch similar tasks together. By grouping tasks that require similar cognitive processes, you can reduce the need to switch between different types of activities. For example, set specific times to check and respond to emails rather than doing it sporadically throughout the day. This way, you can focus entirely on your emails during those periods and then switch to other tasks without lingering thoughts about your inbox.

- **Use Transition Rituals**

Transition rituals are small, intentional activities that signal the end of one task and the beginning of another. These rituals help clear your mind of the previous task and prepare it for the new one. For example, before switching tasks, you could take a few deep breaths, stretch, or jot down a quick note about what you accomplished. These simple actions can help reset your focus and reduce attention residue.

Exercise: Transition Rituals
1. **Identify Transition Points**: Identify points in your day where you typically switch tasks.
2. **Choose a Ritual**: Select a simple ritual to perform at each transition point. This could be deep breathing, stretching, or making a brief note about the completed task.
3. **Practice Consistently**: Make it a habit to perform your chosen ritual each time you switch tasks. Over time, this practice can help reduce attention residue and improve your focus.

- **Limit Multitasking**

Multitasking is one of the primary causes of attention residue. To minimize its impact, reduce the number of tasks you try to juggle at once. Focus on completing one task before moving on to the next. By giving your full attention to one task at a time, you can work more efficiently and produce higher-quality work.

Exercise: Single-Tasking
1. **Prioritize Your Tasks**: At the start of each day, prioritize your tasks and identify which ones require your undivided attention.
2. **Set Boundaries**: Create boundaries to protect your focus. For example, turn off notifications and set specific times to check emails and messages.

3. **Commit to Completion**: Commit to completing each task before moving on to the next. If you get interrupted, make a note of where you left off and quickly return to the task once the interruption is over.

- **Use Focus Tools and Techniques**

There are several tools and techniques designed to help you maintain focus and minimize attention residue. Techniques like the Pomodoro Technique, - we'll discuss more on this later. Additionally, apps like Focus@Will, Forest, and StayFocusd can provide structured environments that support concentration.

Exercise: Implement Focus Tools

1. **Choose a Technique**: Select a focus technique, such as the Pomodoro Technique, to structure your work sessions.
2. **Set Up Your Environment**: Use apps or tools that block distractions and create a conducive environment for focused work.
3. **Follow the Technique**: Adhere to the chosen technique consistently. For example, work for 25 minutes and take a 5-minute break, repeating this cycle throughout your workday.

- **Plan and Schedule Your Day**

Planning and scheduling your day in advance can help you stay on track and reduce the temptation to switch tasks. When you have a clear plan for your day, it's easier to focus on one task at a time and minimize attention residue.

Exercise: Daily Planning

1. **Create a To-Do List**: At the end of each day, create a to-do list for the next day. List all the tasks you need to complete and prioritize them.

2. **Schedule Task Blocks**: Allocate specific time blocks for each task on your list. Ensure that you include breaks and buffer time between tasks.
3. **Review and Adjust**: At the end of the day, review your progress and adjust your plan for the next day as needed. This practice helps you stay organized and focused.

The Long-Term Benefits of Reducing Attention Residue

Minimizing attention residue is not just about improving productivity in the short term. It also has long-term benefits for your mental health and overall well-being. By reducing the constant switching of tasks, you can experience lower stress levels, improved cognitive function, and a greater sense of accomplishment.

- **Lower Stress Levels**

Constantly switching tasks and dealing with attention residue can increase stress levels. By focusing on one task at a time, you can reduce the mental strain and enjoy a more relaxed, stress-free work environment.

- **Improved Cognitive Functions**

Reducing attention residue allows your brain to operate more efficiently. This leads to improved cognitive function, better problem-solving abilities, and enhanced creativity.

- **Greater Sense of Accomplishment**

Completing tasks without the interference of attention residue can give you a greater sense of accomplishment. When you finish a task with full concentration, you can take pride in your work and feel more satisfied with your achievements.

Cognitive Bottlenecks

Cognitive bottlenecks occur when our brain's processing capacity is maxed out, causing a significant slowdown in our ability to think, make decisions, and perform tasks efficiently. Just like a physical bottleneck slows down traffic, cognitive bottlenecks hinder mental processes, leading to reduced productivity and increased errors. Understanding and managing these bottlenecks is essential for maintaining optimal cognitive performance.

The Brain's Processing Capacity

Our brains are incredibly powerful, but they have their limits. The brain can only handle a certain amount of information at a time. When we overload it with multiple tasks, it struggles to process everything efficiently. This results in cognitive bottlenecks, where the flow of information and processing speed are significantly reduced.

To put it simply, imagine a traffic bottleneck. When too many cars try to pass through a narrow road at the same time, traffic slows down, and it takes longer for each car to get through. Similarly, when your brain is trying to process too many tasks or pieces of information at once, it creates a cognitive bottleneck, slowing down your mental processes and reducing your overall efficiency.

Causes of Cognitive Bottlenecks

Several factors can contribute to cognitive bottlenecks, including:

- **Task Overload**
  - Attempting to handle too many tasks at once.
  - The brain's limited capacity to manage multiple complex tasks simultaneously.
- **Information Overload**

- Exposure to excessive amounts of information in a short period.
- Difficulty in filtering and prioritizing relevant information.
- **Frequent Task Switching**
- Constantly switching between tasks, leading to attention residue.
- Increased time and cognitive effort required to refocus.
- **Complexity of Tasks**
- Engaging in tasks that require high levels of cognitive processing.
- The brain's struggle to allocate resources efficiently among complex tasks.

Strategies to Manage Cognitive Bottlenecks

To manage cognitive bottlenecks effectively, it's important to implement strategies that optimize your brain's processing capacity and reduce the likelihood of overload. Here are some practical techniques:

- **Prioritize Tasks**

Focusing on high-priority tasks when your cognitive resources are at their peak can help you manage cognitive bottlenecks. For most people, this is usually in the morning when the brain is fresh and alert.

Exercise: Task Prioritization

1. **List Your Tasks**: Write down all the tasks you need to complete for the day or week.
2. **Identify Priorities**: Rank your tasks based on their importance and urgency. High-priority tasks should be at the top of your list.
3. **Allocate Peak Times**: Schedule high-priority tasks during times when you're most alert and focused. For example, tackle challenging tasks in the morning.

- **Simplify Your Schedule**

Breaking down complex tasks into smaller, manageable chunks can make them easier to handle and reduce cognitive load. This approach allows you to focus on one aspect of a task at a time, minimizing the risk of bottlenecks.

Exercise: Task Simplification

1. **Break Down Tasks**: For each complex task, break it down into smaller, actionable steps. For example, if you have a large project, divide it into specific milestones.
2. **Create a Timeline**: Develop a timeline for completing each step, ensuring that you allocate enough time for each part of the task.
3. **Focus on One Step at a Time**: Concentrate on completing one step before moving on to the next. This helps maintain focus and reduces cognitive strain.

- **Take Regular Breaks**

Giving your brain time to rest and recover is crucial for maintaining cognitive performance and preventing bottlenecks. Short breaks throughout the day can help refresh your mind and enhance your ability to concentrate.

Exercise: Implementing Breaks

1. **Schedule Breaks**: Plan regular breaks into your daily schedule. For example, use the Pomodoro Technique, working for 25 minutes and then taking a 5-minute break.
2. **Relax and Recharge**: During breaks, engage in activities that help you relax and recharge. This could be stretching, walking, or practicing mindfulness.
3. **Avoid Digital Distractions**: Use your breaks to disconnect from digital devices and reduce cognitive overload.

- **Use Cognitive Offloading**

Cognitive offloading involves using external tools and resources to manage information and tasks, reducing the cognitive burden on your brain. This can include writing things down, using calendars, and leveraging technology.

Exercise: Cognitive Offloading Techniques

1. **Write It Down**: Use a notebook or digital app to jot down important information, tasks, and ideas. This frees up mental space and reduces the risk of forgetting.
2. **Use Calendars and Reminders**: Set up calendars and reminders for important tasks and deadlines. This helps you stay organized and reduces cognitive load.
3. **Leverage Technology**: Utilize productivity tools and apps to manage your tasks and information efficiently. For example, use task management apps like Todoist or Trello.

Yes, I remember the writing style you prefer. It should be conversational, similar to Brian Tracy's, making the content engaging and relatable while being clear and direct. The language needs to be simple enough for a 10-year-old to understand but aimed at young adults and adults. Let's dive into mastering sequential focus, covering chunking and batching, and the Pomodoro Technique in detail.

Chunking and Batching

Chunking and batching are powerful techniques that can transform the way you manage tasks and enhance your focus. By breaking down tasks into smaller parts and grouping similar tasks together, you can work more efficiently and reduce cognitive overload.

What is Chunking?

Chunking is a method of breaking down large tasks or pieces of information into smaller, more manageable units or "chunks." This technique leverages our brain's natural ability to process information in bite-sized pieces, making it easier to understand, remember, and complete tasks.

A classic example of chunking is how we remember phone numbers. Instead of trying to remember a string of 10 digits, we break it down into chunks: (123) 456-7890. This same principle can be applied to tasks and projects.

How to Apply Chunking

1. **Identify the Task**: Start with a large task or project that feels overwhelming.
2. **Break It Down**: Divide the task into smaller, manageable chunks. For example, if you need to write a report, break it down into sections such as research, outline, first draft, and final edit.
3. **Prioritize Chunks**: Arrange the chunks in a logical order, prioritizing the most critical parts first.
4. **Set Deadlines**: Assign deadlines to each chunk to ensure steady progress and prevent procrastination.

Exercise: Chunking a Project

1. **Select a Project**: Choose a project you need to complete, such as planning an event or writing a research paper.
2. **List Major Components**: Write down the main components of the project. For planning an event, components might include venue selection, invitations, catering, and entertainment.
3. **Break Down Components**: For each component, list the smaller tasks required. For venue selection, tasks could include researching venues, visiting sites, and booking the venue.

4. **Create a Timeline**: Assign deadlines to each smaller task to ensure you stay on track and complete the project on time.

What is Batching?

Batching is the process of grouping similar tasks together and completing them in one dedicated session. This technique minimizes the cognitive cost of task-switching and allows you to maintain focus on a specific type of work. By batching similar tasks, you reduce the number of switches and allow your brain to stay in one mode for a longer period.

How to Apply Batching

1. **Identify Similar Tasks**: List out tasks that are similar in nature. This could be emails, phone calls, administrative work, or creative tasks.
2. **Schedule Batch Sessions**: Allocate specific times in your calendar for these batch sessions. For example, set aside an hour in the morning to handle all emails and another hour in the afternoon for phone calls.
3. **Minimize Distractions**: During your batch sessions, eliminate distractions and focus solely on the tasks at hand.

Exercise: Batching Daily Tasks

1. **List Daily Tasks**: Write down all the tasks you need to complete in a typical day.
2. **Group Similar Tasks**: Group tasks that are similar. For example, batch all your emails, social media updates, and administrative tasks together.
3. **Create a Schedule**: Allocate specific time blocks for each batch of tasks. Ensure you stick to this schedule to maintain focus and efficiency.

Examples of Chunking and Batching in Practice

1. **Writing a Book**: An author can use chunking to break the book into chapters and then further into sections or scenes. Batching can be applied by dedicating specific days to writing, editing, and researching.
2. **Managing Emails**: Instead of checking emails constantly, set specific times during the day to batch process emails. This reduces interruptions and allows you to respond more efficiently.
3. **Household Chores**: Group similar chores together, such as cleaning all the rooms or doing all the laundry in one go. This saves time and effort compared to doing them sporadically.

The Pomodoro Technique

The Pomodoro Technique is a time management method developed by Francesco Cirillo in the late 1980s. It involves breaking work into intervals, traditionally 25 minutes in length, separated by short breaks. These intervals are known as "Pomodoros."

The Pomodoro Technique leverages the idea that frequent breaks can improve mental agility. By working in short, focused bursts and taking regular breaks, you can maintain high levels of productivity and reduce the risk of burnout.

How to Apply the Pomodoro Technique

1. **Choose a Task**: Select a task you want to work on.
2. **Set a Timer**: Set a timer for 25 minutes. During this time, focus solely on the task at hand.
3. **Work Until the Timer Rings**: Work on the task without any interruptions until the timer rings.

4. **Take a Short Break**: Take a 5-minute break to rest and recharge. Use this time to stretch, walk around, or do something relaxing.
5. **Repeat the Process**: After four Pomodoros, take a longer break of 15-30 minutes to give your brain a more substantial rest.

Benefits of the Pomodoro Technique

- **Enhanced Focus**: The 25-minute work intervals help maintain concentration and prevent distractions.
- **Regular Breaks**: The frequent breaks help refresh your mind and maintain cognitive performance throughout the day.
- **Reduced Procrastination**: The short work intervals make it easier to start tasks and reduce the tendency to procrastinate.
- **Improved Time Management**: The structured approach helps you manage your time effectively and ensure that you allocate enough time for each task.

Exercise: Implementing the Pomodoro Technique

1. **Select a Task**: Choose a task that you need to focus on.
2. **Set Up a Timer**: Use a timer app or a physical timer to track your Pomodoro sessions.
3. **Work for 25 Minutes**: Focus solely on the task for 25 minutes, avoiding all distractions.
4. **Take a 5-Minute Break**: After the timer rings, take a short break to relax and recharge.
5. **Repeat and Reflect**: Repeat the process and, at the end of the day, reflect on how the Pomodoro Technique affected your focus and productivity.

Advanced Techniques with the Pomodoro Method

Once you're comfortable with the basics of the Pomodoro Technique, you can experiment with advanced techniques to further enhance your productivity.

1. **Customize Your Intervals**: While the standard Pomodoro interval is 25 minutes, you can adjust the length to fit your personal preferences and the nature of your tasks. For example, some people find that 45-minute intervals work better for deep work.
2. **Track Your Pomodoros**: Keep a log of your completed Pomodoros. This helps you track your progress, identify patterns, and make adjustments as needed.
3. **Group Similar Tasks**: Use the Pomodoro Technique in conjunction with batching by grouping similar tasks and completing them in Pomodoro intervals.

Exercise: Advanced Pomodoro Techniques

1. **Experiment with Intervals**: Try different interval lengths, such as 20, 30, or 45 minutes, to find what works best for you.
2. **Log Your Sessions**: Keep a log of your Pomodoro sessions, noting the tasks completed and any observations about your focus and productivity.
3. **Combine with Batching**: Group similar tasks and use the Pomodoro Technique to complete them in focused intervals.

Combining Chunking, Batching, and the Pomodoro Technique

Chunking, batching, and the Pomodoro Technique are not mutually exclusive. In fact, they can be combined to create a highly effective workflow.

1. **Chunking with Pomodoros**: Break large tasks into smaller chunks and complete each chunk in a Pomodoro session. This helps you maintain focus and make consistent progress.
2. **Batching with Pomodoros**: Batch similar tasks and complete them using the Pomodoro Technique. For example, batch all your emails and process them in several Pomodoro intervals.
3. **Optimize Your Workflow**: Use chunking to break down projects, batching to group similar tasks, and the Pomodoro Technique to manage your time effectively. This comprehensive approach can maximize productivity and minimize cognitive overload.

Exercise: Combining Techniques

1. **Select a Project**: Choose a project you need to complete.
2. **Chunk the Project**: Break the project into smaller chunks.
3. **Batch Similar Tasks**: Group similar tasks within the project.
4. **Apply the Pomodoro Technique**: Complete each chunk and batch using the Pomodoro Technique, working in focused intervals with regular breaks.

Case Study: Implementing Sequential Focus Techniques

Let's consider the example of Anabelle, a marketing manager, who needs to create a comprehensive marketing plan for her company.

1. **Chunking the Project:**

- Anabelle breaks down the marketing plan into smaller chunks: market research, strategy development, content creation, and campaign planning.
2. **Batching Similar Tasks:**
- She identifies similar tasks within each chunk. For market research, she batches tasks such as competitor analysis, customer surveys, and data collection.
3. **Using the Pomodoro Technique:**
- Anabelle schedules specific Pomodoro sessions for each batch of tasks. She sets a timer for 25 minutes and focuses solely on competitor analysis. After 25 minutes, she takes a 5-minute break and then moves on to the next task in the batch.
4. **Tracking Progress:**
- Anabelle keeps a log of her Pomodoro sessions, noting the tasks completed and her observations on focus and productivity. This helps her identify any adjustments needed to optimize her workflow.
5. **Reflecting on Results:**
- At the end of the week, Anabelle reflects on her progress. She finds that chunking, batching, and using the Pomodoro Technique have significantly improved her focus and productivity. She feels less overwhelmed and more in control of her workload.

The 80/20 Rule (Pareto Principle)

The 80/20 Rule, also known as the Pareto Principle, is a powerful concept that can dramatically improve your productivity and help you overcome procrastination. Named after the Italian economist Vilfredo Pareto, the principle suggests that roughly 80% of your results come from 20% of your efforts. In other words, a small portion of your activities accounts for the majority of your outcomes. By identifying and focusing on these high-impact tasks, you can maximize your efficiency and make significant progress toward your goals.

Understanding The Pareto Principle

The Pareto Principle is based on the observation that resources are often distributed unevenly. For instance, in Pareto's original study, he found that 80% of the land in Italy was owned by 20% of the population. This principle can be applied to various areas of life, including business, personal productivity, and time management. In the context of overcoming procrastination, the Pareto Principle helps you prioritize tasks that will yield the most significant results.

Key Concepts of the Pareto Principle:

1. **Focus on the Vital Few**: Identify the few tasks or activities that have the greatest impact on your goals.
2. **Eliminate or Delegate the Trivial Many**: Reduce, eliminate, or delegate tasks that contribute little to your overall success.
3. **Maximize Your Efforts**: Concentrate your time and energy on high-impact activities to achieve the best results.

Applying the Pareto Principle to Overcome Procrastination

To effectively apply the Pareto Principle, you need to identify your most important tasks and focus your efforts on completing them. This approach helps you avoid wasting time on low-value activities and reduces the tendency to procrastinate on critical tasks.

Step 1: Identify High-Impact Tasks

Begin by identifying the tasks that have the most significant impact on your goals. These are the tasks that contribute the most value and are essential for your success.

Exercise: Task Identification

1. **List Your Tasks**: Write down all the tasks you need to complete. Include both work-related and personal tasks.
2. **Evaluate Impact: Assess the impact of each task on your goals. Consider** factors such as how much progress the task will help you make, its importance, and its urgency.
3. **Rank Tasks**: Rank the tasks based on their impact. Identify the top 20% of tasks that will produce 80% of your desired results.

Example: If you are a student, your list might include tasks like studying for exams, completing assignments, attending classes, and participating in extracurricular activities. After evaluating their impact, you might rank studying for exams and completing assignments as the highest-impact tasks.

Step 2: Prioritize High-Impact Tasks

Once you have identified the high-impact tasks, prioritize them in your daily and weekly schedule. Ensure that you allocate sufficient time and resources to complete these tasks.

Exercise: Prioritization

1. **Create a Task Hierarchy**: Organize your high-impact tasks into a hierarchy based on their importance and urgency.
2. **Set Priorities**: Assign priorities to each task. For example, use labels like "High Priority," "Medium Priority," and "Low Priority."
3. **Allocate Time**: Schedule specific time blocks in your calendar to work on high-priority tasks. Ensure that these time blocks are free from distractions.

Example: Continuing with the student example, you might prioritize studying for an upcoming exam over completing a less urgent assignment. You would then schedule dedicated study sessions in your calendar.

Step 3: Eliminate or Delegate Low-Impact Tasks

To maximize your productivity, it's essential to minimize the time spent on low-impact tasks. This can involve eliminating unnecessary tasks or delegating them to others.

Exercise: Task Elimination and Delegation

1. **Identify Low-Impact Tasks**: Review your task list and identify tasks that have minimal impact on your goals.
2. **Consider Elimination**: Determine if any of these tasks can be eliminated without significant consequences. Remove them from your list if possible.
3. **Delegate Where Possible**: Identify tasks that can be delegated to others. Consider delegating routine or administrative tasks to free up time for high-impact activities.

Example: If managing social media is a low-impact task for you, consider delegating it to a virtual assistant or using automation tools to reduce the time spent on it.

Step 4: Focus on One Task at a Time

Multitasking can dilute your efforts and reduce the effectiveness of your work. By focusing on one high-impact task at a time, you can achieve better results and reduce procrastination.

Example: If you have prioritized studying for an exam, set a clear objective, such as reviewing a specific chapter. Work in focused intervals, taking breaks to maintain your concentration and avoid burnout.

Step 5: Review and Adjust

Regularly reviewing your progress and adjusting your approach is crucial for maintaining productivity. This ensures that you remain focused on high-impact tasks and continue to make meaningful progress.

Exercise: Progress Review

1. **Weekly Review**: At the end of each week, review the tasks you have completed. Assess whether they were high-impact and contributed to your goals.
2. **Reflect on Challenges**: Identify any challenges or obstacles you encountered. Consider how you can address these challenges in the future.
3. **Adjust Priorities**: Based on your review, adjust your task priorities for the upcoming week. Ensure that you continue to focus on high-impact tasks.

Example: During your weekly review, you might realize that you spent too much time on low-impact activities. Adjust your schedule for the next week to allocate more time to high-impact tasks and reduce or eliminate low-impact ones.

Adopting a Single-Tasking Mindset

Shifting from a multitasking mentality to a single-tasking approach requires overcoming common barriers such as the Fear of Missing Out (FOMO) and embracing monotasking as a more effective way to manage tasks and responsibilities.

Overcoming FOMO

Fear of Missing Out, or FOMO, is a pervasive feeling that something important is happening elsewhere and you are not part of it. This fear can drive the constant need to check emails, social media, and messages, leading to fragmented attention and reduced productivity.

FOMO is rooted in the fear that we are missing out on valuable information, opportunities, or social interactions. In the context of work, it might manifest as the need to stay updated with emails, attend every meeting, or respond immediately to every message. While staying informed and connected is important, constantly giving in to FOMO can significantly hinder your ability to focus and complete tasks efficiently.

Strategies to Overcome FOMO

Overcoming FOMO involves changing your mindset and implementing practical strategies to stay focused and present.

- **Set Clear Priorities**

Having clear priorities helps you focus on what truly matters, reducing the urge to check every notification or email.

Exercise: Prioritization Matrix

1. **List Your Tasks**: Write down all your tasks for the day.
2. **Categorize Tasks**: Use a prioritization matrix to categorize tasks based on their urgency and importance.
   - ☐ **Urgent and Important**: High-priority tasks that need immediate attention.
   - ☐ **Important but Not Urgent**: Tasks that are important but can be scheduled for later.
   - ☐ **Urgent but Not Important**: Tasks that require immediate attention but are not critical.
   - ☐ **Not Urgent and Not Important**: Low-priority tasks that can be delegated or eliminated.
3. **Focus on High-Priority** Tasks: Allocate your time and energy to high-priority tasks, ensuring that you stay focused on what matters most.

- **Limit Notifications**

Reducing the number of notifications you receive can significantly decrease distractions and help you stay focused on your tasks.

Exercise: Notification Management

1. **Audit Your Notifications**: Review the notifications you receive on your devices. Identify which ones are necessary and which ones are not.
2. **Turn Off Unnecessary Notifications**: Disable notifications for non-essential apps and channels. For example, turn off social media notifications during work hours.
3. **Set Notification Rules**: Establish specific times to check notifications, such as during scheduled breaks or after completing a task.

- **Practice Mindfulness**

Mindfulness practices can help you stay present and reduce the anxiety associated with FOMO.

Exercise: Mindfulness Meditation

1. **Find a Quiet Space**: Choose a quiet, comfortable space to practice mindfulness meditation.
2. **Focus on Your Breath:** Close your eyes and focus on your breath. Notice the sensation of the air entering and leaving your body.
3. **Acknowledge and Let Go of Thoughts**: When thoughts about missing out arise, acknowledge them without judgment and gently bring your focus back to your breath.
4. **Practice Regularly**: Incorporate mindfulness meditation into your daily routine to strengthen your ability to stay present.

- **Create a Digital Detox Routine**

A digital detox involves setting aside time to disconnect from digital devices and reduce the constant influx of information.

Exercise: Digital Detox

1. **Schedule Detox Periods**: Allocate specific times each day or week for a digital detox. During this time, avoid using digital devices and focus on offline activities.
2. **Engage in Offline Activities**: Use this time to engage in activities that do not involve screens, such as reading a book, going for a walk, or spending time with loved ones.
3. **Reflect on the Experience**: Reflect on how the digital detox affects your focus, stress levels, and overall well-being.

- **Develop a Growth Mindset**

Adopting a growth mindset can help you see the value in focusing on a single task and reducing the need to constantly check for new information.

Exercise: Growth Mindset Affirmations

1. **Identify Limiting Beliefs**: Identify any beliefs that contribute to FOMO, such as "I need to stay updated all the time" or "I might miss something important."
2. **Create Affirmations**: Develop positive affirmations that counter these limiting beliefs. For example, "I am focused and productive when I dedicate my full attention to one task" or "I trust that I will receive important information at the right time."
3. **Repeat Affirmations Daily**: Incorporate these affirmations into your daily routine to reinforce a growth mindset and reduce FOMO.

Embracing Monotasking

Monotasking, or single-tasking, involves dedicating your full attention to one task at a time. Embracing monotasking requires a shift in mindset and the adoption of strategies that support focused work.

Strategies to Embrace Monotasking

To embrace monotasking, it is essential to adopt practical strategies that support focused work and minimize distractions.

- **Implement the Two-Minute Rule**

The two-minute rule involves immediately completing any task that can be done in two minutes or less. This helps you clear small tasks quickly, reducing the mental load and allowing you to focus on more significant tasks.

Exercise: Applying the Two-Minute Rule

1. **Identify Small Tasks**: Throughout your day, identify tasks that can be completed in two minutes or less.
2. **Complete Immediately**: Complete these small tasks immediately rather than letting them accumulate. This helps you clear your mind and maintain focus on larger tasks.
3. **Reflect on Efficiency**: Reflect on how applying the two-minute rule affects your productivity and focus. Adjust your approach as needed to optimize efficiency.

- **Develop a Shutdown Routine**

A shutdown routine is a series of activities you perform at the end of your workday to signal that work is over. This helps you mentally disconnect from work and transition to personal time.

Exercise: Creating a Shutdown Routine

1. **Review Your Day**: At the end of your workday, review the tasks you completed and any outstanding tasks that need attention.
2. **Plan for Tomorrow**: Create a to-do list for the next day, prioritizing tasks and allocating time blocks.
3. **Organize Your Workspace**: Tidy up your workspace and prepare it for the next day.

4. **Engage in a Relaxing Activity**: Choose an activity that helps you unwind, such as reading, meditating, or spending time with loved ones.
5. **Reflect on Your Routine**: Reflect on how the shutdown routine affects your ability to disconnect from work and recharge. Make any necessary adjustments to enhance its effectiveness.

- **Embrace the Power of Saying No**

Learning to say no to non-essential tasks and distractions is crucial for maintaining focus and embracing monotasking.

Exercise: Saying No

1. **Identify Non-Essential Tasks**: Review your tasks and commitments to identify non-essential activities that can be eliminated or delegated.
2. **Set Boundaries**: Communicate your boundaries to colleagues, friends, and family. Let them know when you are unavailable for interruptions.
3. **Practice Assertiveness**: Practice saying no politely but firmly to requests that do not align with your priorities. For example, "I appreciate the offer, but I need to focus on my current project right now."
4. **Reflect on Your Boundaries**: Reflect on how setting boundaries and saying no affects your focus and productivity. Adjust your approach as needed to maintain a balance between work and personal life.

- **Foster a Single-Tasking Culture**

Promoting a single-tasking culture in your workplace or personal life can create an environment that supports focused work.

Exercise: Promoting Single-Tasking

1. **Lead by Example**: Model single-tasking behavior by focusing on one task at a time and avoiding multitasking.

2. **Encourage Colleagues**: Encourage colleagues to adopt single-tasking practices, such as time blocking and deep work sessions.
3. **Create a Supportive Environment**: Establish guidelines and practices that support focused work, such as minimizing unnecessary meetings and interruptions.
4. **Reflect on the Culture**: Reflect on how promoting a single-tasking culture affects the overall productivity and well-being of your team or household.

Key Takeaways

1. Single-tasking enhances productivity by allowing full concentration on one task at a time.
2. Attention residue from frequent task switching hinders performance and increases errors.
3. Cognitive bottlenecks occur when the brain is overwhelmed with too much information at once, reducing efficiency.
4. Overcoming FOMO and embracing monotasking requires setting clear priorities and boundaries.
5. Adopting single-tasking habits, like using the Pomodoro Technique and establishing routines, supports focused work.

Reflective Questions

1. How often do you find yourself switching between tasks, and what impact does it have on your productivity?
2. What are some small tasks you can immediately complete using the two-minute rule to clear mental space?
3. How can you create a shutdown routine that helps you transition from work to personal time effectively?
4. What strategies can you implement to reduce FOMO and enhance your focus on single tasks?

5. In what ways can you promote a single-tasking culture within your team or household to support better focus and productivity?

CHAPTER 6
Energy Management

Energy management is an essential component of productivity that is often overlooked. While time management focuses on how you allocate your hours, energy management is about optimizing your physical, emotional, and mental energy to perform tasks effectively. Understanding and managing your energy can help you maintain high levels of productivity, avoid burnout, and achieve a better balance between work and personal life.

In this chapter, discuss principles of energy management and explore how understanding your energy cycles can lead to better performance and overall well-being. We will start also looking into how to optimize your energy and recharge.

Introduction to Energy Management

Energy management is about making conscious decisions to optimize your energy levels throughout the day. It involves recognizing when you have the most energy, aligning your most demanding tasks with these periods, and ensuring you recharge effectively during downtimes.

Why Energy Management Matters

Effective energy management is crucial for several reasons:

1. **Sustained Productivity**: By managing your energy, you can sustain high levels of productivity throughout the day without experiencing significant dips in performance.
2. **Improved Quality of Work**: When you align your tasks with your energy levels, you can produce higher quality work because you're working at your peak capacity.

3. **Reduced Stress and Burnout**: Proper energy management helps you avoid burnout by ensuring you take regular breaks and recharge effectively.
4. **Better Work-Life Balance**: Managing your energy allows you to be more present and engaged in both your professional and personal life.

Components of Energy Management

Energy management can be broken down into four main components:

1. **Physical Energy**: This includes your overall health, fitness, and physical well-being. Factors such as diet, exercise, and sleep play a significant role in maintaining physical energy.
2. **Emotional Energy**: Your emotional state can greatly impact your energy levels. Managing stress, maintaining positive relationships, and finding emotional outlets are crucial for sustaining emotional energy.
3. **Mental Energy**: Cognitive tasks and mental workload require significant energy. Effective planning, prioritization, and minimizing distractions can help manage mental energy.
4. **Spiritual Energy**: This involves a sense of purpose and alignment with your values and goals. Engaging in activities that are meaningful and fulfilling can enhance your spiritual energy.

Strategies for Effective Energy Management

1. **Regular Breaks**: Taking regular breaks throughout the day helps recharge your energy levels and maintain focus.
2. **Healthy Lifestyle**: Adopting a healthy lifestyle that includes proper nutrition, regular exercise, and sufficient sleep supports physical energy.

3. **Stress Management**: Techniques such as mindfulness, meditation, and relaxation exercises can help manage stress and sustain emotional energy.
4. **Task Prioritization**: Aligning your most demanding tasks with your peak energy periods ensures you're working at your best when it matters most.

Understanding Energy Cycles

Energy cycles refer to the natural fluctuations in your energy levels throughout the day. By understanding these cycles, you can optimize your tasks and activities to match your peak performance periods. One key concept in understanding energy cycles is ultradian rhythms.

Ultradian Rhythms

Ultradian rhythms are recurrent periods or cycles repeated throughout a 24-hour day. These cycles, which typically last 90-120 minutes, are characterized by alternating periods of high and low energy. Understanding ultradian rhythms can help you optimize your work patterns and maintain peak performance.

Ultradian rhythms are part of your body's natural biological clock, known as the circadian rhythm. While the circadian rhythm regulates your sleep-wake cycle over a 24-hour period, ultradian rhythms occur multiple times throughout the day and influence your energy levels, alertness, and cognitive performance.

Key Features of Ultradian Rhythms

1. **90-120 Minute Cycles**: Ultradian rhythms typically last between 90 and 120 minutes. During this time, your energy levels rise to a peak and then gradually decline.

2. **Rest and Recovery**: After a peak period, your body needs a brief period of rest and recovery, usually lasting around 20 minutes, before it can enter another high-energy phase.
3. **Biological Basis**: Ultradian rhythms are driven by underlying biological processes, including hormone levels, brain wave activity, and cellular function.

Identifying Your Ultradian Rhythms

Understanding your ultradian rhythms can help you align your tasks with your natural energy cycles. Here are some steps to identify your ultradian rhythms:

1. **Observe Your Energy Levels**: Pay attention to your energy levels throughout the day. Note when you feel most alert and when you experience dips in energy.
2. **Track Your Cycles**: Use a journal or an app to track your energy levels over several days. Look for patterns in your energy fluctuations.
3. **Identify Peak Periods**: Identify the times of day when you consistently feel most energetic and focused. These are your peak periods.

Exercise: Tracking Ultradian Rhythms

1. **Energy Journal**: Keep an energy journal for one week. Record your energy levels every hour, noting how alert or fatigued you feel.
2. **Analyze Patterns**: At the end of the week, analyze your journal to identify patterns in your energy levels. Look for recurring high-energy and low-energy periods.
3. **Align Tasks**: Use this information to align your most demanding tasks with your peak energy periods and schedule breaks during low-energy times.

Identifying Peak Periods

Identifying your peak periods is crucial for optimizing your energy management strategy. Peak periods are the times of day when you naturally have the most energy, focus, and cognitive function. By aligning your most demanding tasks with these periods, you can maximize your productivity and performance.

How to Identify Peak Periods

1. **Self-Observation**: Pay attention to your energy levels throughout the day. Notice when you feel most alert and productive and when you experience energy slumps.
2. **Energy Tracking**: Use an energy tracking tool or journal to monitor your energy levels over several days or weeks. Record your energy levels at regular intervals and look for patterns.
3. **Reflect on Past Performance**: Reflect on times when you have performed at your best. What time of day was it? What were the conditions? Use this information to identify your peak periods.

Exercise: Identifying Peak Periods

1. **Energy Tracking Journal**: Keep an energy-tracking journal for two weeks. Record your energy levels at regular intervals, such as every hour.
2. **Analyze Data**: At the end of the tracking period, analyze your data to identify patterns and trends. Look for recurring times when you feel most energetic and focused.
3. **Confirm Peak Periods**: Confirm your peak periods by reflecting on your past performance and considering any external factors that may influence your energy levels.

Aligning Tasks with Peak Periods

Once you have identified your peak periods, it is important to align your tasks and activities with these times to optimize your productivity.

- **Schedule High-Priority Tasks**

Schedule your most important and demanding tasks during your peak periods. This ensures that you are working on these tasks when you are most alert and capable of performing at your best.

Exercise: Task Scheduling

1. **List High-Priority Tasks**: Make a list of your high-priority tasks and projects.
2. **Allocate Peak Periods**: Allocate your peak periods to these high-priority tasks. Ensure that you have sufficient time to complete them without interruptions.
3. **Protect Your Time**: Set boundaries to protect your peak periods from unnecessary meetings, interruptions, or distractions.

- **Plan Low-Energy Activities**

Plan lighter, less demanding activities during your low-energy periods. These activities might include administrative tasks, routine work, or tasks that require less cognitive effort.

Exercise: Planning Low-Energy Activities

1. **Identify Low-Energy Tasks**: Make a list of tasks that require less energy and focus.
2. **Allocate Low-Energy Periods**: Schedule these tasks during your low-energy periods. This allows you to use these times productively without overexerting yourself.
3. **Take Breaks**: Incorporate short breaks during low-energy periods to rest and recharge. This helps you maintain overall energy levels throughout the day.

- **Create a Balanced Schedule**

Creating a balanced schedule that aligns with your energy levels helps you maintain productivity and well-being throughout the day.

Exercise: Balanced Scheduling

1. **Divide Your Day**: Divide your day into blocks based on your energy levels. Allocate peak periods for high-priority tasks, low-energy periods for lighter tasks, and include regular breaks.
2. **Review and Adjust**: Regularly review your schedule and make adjustments as needed to ensure it aligns with your energy levels and priorities.
3. **Reflect on Performance**: Reflect on your performance and well-being at the end of each day. Adjust your schedule based on what works best for you.

Practical Strategies for Energy Management

To effectively manage your energy, it is important to adopt practical strategies that support your physical, emotional, mental, and spiritual well-being. Here are some key strategies to consider:

1. **Optimize Physical Energy**
- **Healthy Diet**: Eat a balanced diet rich in nutrients to fuel your body and maintain steady energy levels.
- **Regular Exercise**: Incorporate regular physical activity into your routine to boost energy, improve mood, and enhance cognitive function.
- **Quality Sleep**: Prioritize quality sleep by establishing a consistent sleep schedule and creating a restful sleep environment.
- **Hydration**: Stay hydrated throughout the day to maintain optimal physical and cognitive performance.
2. **Support Emotional Energy**

- Stress Management: Practice stress management techniques such as mindfulness, meditation, and relaxation exercises to reduce stress and maintain emotional balance.
- Positive Relationships: Cultivate positive relationships and social connections to support your emotional well-being.
- Emotional Outlets: Find healthy outlets for expressing and processing emotions, such as journaling, creative activities, or talking to a trusted friend.

3. **Enhance Mental Energy**
- Task Prioritization: Prioritize tasks and focus on high-priority activities during your peak energy periods.
- Minimize Distractions: Minimize distractions by creating a focused work environment and setting boundaries with others.
- Mental Breaks: Take regular mental breaks to rest and recharge your cognitive resources.

4. **Foster Spiritual Energy**
- Purpose and Meaning: Engage in activities that align with your values and provide a sense of purpose and meaning.
- Reflection and Gratitude: Practice reflection and gratitude to cultivate a positive mindset and enhance spiritual well-being.
- Mindful Living: Incorporate mindfulness practices into your daily life to stay present and connected to your inner self.

Optimizing Your Energy

Optimizing your energy is about making deliberate choices to maintain high levels of physical, mental, and emotional vitality throughout the day. Optimizing your energy means being aware of and actively managing the factors that influence your vitality. It's about recognizing that your body and mind have natural rhythms and limitations and that by working with these rhythms, you can enhance your performance and well-being.

The Importance of Optimizing Energy

1. **Sustained Productivity**: By managing your energy, you can maintain consistent productivity levels throughout the day without experiencing significant energy slumps.
2. **Improved Focus and Concentration**: High energy levels enable better focus and concentration, leading to higher-quality work.
3. **Enhanced Well-Being**: Proper energy management contributes to overall physical and mental health, reducing the risk of burnout and fatigue.
4. **Balanced Lifestyle**: Effective energy management helps balance work and personal life, allowing you to be more present and engaged in all areas of your life.

Components of Energy Optimization

Energy optimization can be broadly categorized into four main components:

1. **Sleep and Recovery**: Ensuring adequate rest and recovery to recharge your physical and mental energy.
2. **Exercise and Nutrition**: Maintaining a healthy lifestyle through regular physical activity and balanced nutrition to support overall vitality.
3. **Mental and Emotional Health**: Managing stress and maintaining positive mental and emotional states to sustain energy levels.
4. **Lifestyle and Habits**: Adopting daily habits and routines that support sustained energy and productivity.

Sleep and Recovery

Sleep and recovery are fundamental to optimizing energy. Sleep is when your body and mind repair, regenerate and prepare for the next day. Recovery includes activities that help you recharge and manage stress, ensuring you are ready to face new challenges.

Sleep is a complex biological process essential for physical health, cognitive function, and emotional well-being. It consists of several stages, each playing a critical role in maintaining overall health.

Stages of Sleep

1. **NREM Sleep (Non-Rapid Eye Movement):**
   - **Stage 1**: Light sleep, where you drift in and out of sleep.
   - **Stage 2**: Slightly deeper sleep, where your body temperature drops and heart rate slows.
   - **Stage 3**: Deep sleep, crucial for physical restoration and growth.
2. **REM Sleep (Rapid Eye Movement):**
   - This stage is vital for cognitive functions such as memory consolidation, learning, and emotional regulation. It is characterized by vivid dreaming and increased brain activity.

The Importance of Sleep

Adequate sleep is essential for:

1. **Physical Health**: Sleep supports immune function, cell repair, and muscle growth. It also regulates hormones that control hunger, stress, and metabolism.
2. **Cognitive Function**: Sleep enhances memory, learning, and problem-solving abilities. It helps clear metabolic waste from the brain, which can affect cognitive performance.

3. **Emotional Well-Being**: Sleep helps regulate emotions and mood, reducing the risk of mental health issues such as anxiety and depression.

Optimizing Sleep for Energy

To optimize your sleep for better energy levels, consider the following strategies:

- **Establish a Consistent Sleep Schedule**

Maintaining a regular sleep schedule helps regulate your body's internal clock, making it easier to fall asleep and wake up at the same time each day.

Exercise: Setting a Sleep Schedule

1. **Choose Bedtime and Wake Time**: Decide on a consistent bedtime and wake time, even on weekends.
2. **Stick to the Schedule**: Commit to going to bed and waking up at the chosen times. Use alarms and bedtime reminders if needed.
3. **Adjust Gradually**: If your current sleep schedule is significantly different from your ideal one, adjust it gradually by 15-30 minutes each day until you reach the desired times.
- **Create a Sleep-Conducive Environment**

Your sleep environment plays a significant role in the quality of your sleep. A comfortable and relaxing sleep space can enhance sleep quality.

Exercise: Optimizing Your Sleep Environment

1. **Dark and Quiet**: Ensure your bedroom is dark and quiet. Use blackout curtains, earplugs, or a white noise machine if needed.

2. **Comfortable Bedding**: Invest in a comfortable mattress and pillows that support good sleep posture.
3. **Cool Temperature**: Keep your bedroom cool, ideally between 60-67°F (15-19°C), to facilitate better sleep.
4. **Minimize Distractions**: Remove or minimize potential distractions, such as electronic devices, from your sleep environment.

- **Practice Good Sleep Hygiene**

Good sleep hygiene involves adopting habits that promote better sleep quality and consistency.

Exercise: Sleep Hygiene Checklist

1. **Limit Screen Time**: Avoid screens at least an hour before bedtime, as the blue light emitted can disrupt your sleep cycle.
2. **Relaxing Bedtime Routine**: Develop a relaxing pre-sleep routine, such as reading, meditating, or taking a warm bath.
3. **Avoid Stimulants**: Avoid caffeine, nicotine, and heavy meals close to bedtime, as they can interfere with sleep.
4. **Physical Activity**: Engage in regular physical activity, but avoid vigorous exercise close to bedtime.

Exercise and Nutrition

Exercise and nutrition are critical components of energy optimization. Regular physical activity and a balanced diet provide the fuel and stamina needed to maintain high energy levels throughout the day.

The Role of Exercise in Energy Optimization

Exercise has numerous benefits that contribute to overall energy levels, including:

1. **Improved Physical Health**: Regular exercise enhances cardiovascular health, muscle strength, and endurance.

2. **Increased Energy Levels**: Physical activity boosts energy by improving circulation and oxygen delivery to tissues.
3. **Enhanced Mood**: Exercise stimulates the release of endorphins, which improve mood and reduce stress.
4. **Better Sleep**: Regular physical activity can improve sleep quality and help regulate sleep patterns.

Types of Exercise for Energy Optimization

Incorporating a variety of exercises into your routine can help optimize energy levels.

- **Cardiovascular Exercise**

Cardiovascular exercise, or cardio, improves heart and lung function, increasing overall stamina and energy.

Exercise: Cardio Activities

1. **Walking or Jogging**: Incorporate brisk walking or jogging into your daily routine.
2. **Cycling**: Engage in cycling, either outdoors or on a stationary bike.
3. **Swimming**: Swimming is an excellent low-impact cardio exercise that improves cardiovascular health.

- **Strength Training**

Strength training builds muscle mass, increases metabolism, and enhances overall physical strength.

Exercise: Strength Training Activities

1. **Bodyweight Exercises**: Perform bodyweight exercises such as push-ups, squats, and lunges.
2. **Weightlifting**: Incorporate weightlifting exercises using dumbbells, barbells, or resistance bands.

3. **Functional Training**: Engage in functional training exercises that mimic everyday movements, such as kettlebell swings and medicine ball throws.
- **Flexibility and Balance Exercises**

Flexibility and balance exercises improve mobility, reduce the risk of injury, and enhance overall physical function.

Exercise: Flexibility and Balance Activities

1. **Yoga**: Practice yoga to improve flexibility, balance, and mental focus.
2. **Stretching**: Incorporate stretching exercises into your routine to enhance flexibility.
3. **Pilates**: Engage in Pilates to strengthen core muscles and improve balance.

Creating an Exercise Routine

Developing a consistent exercise routine tailored to your needs and preferences is key to optimizing energy.

Exercise: Designing Your Exercise Routine

1. **Set Clear Goals**: Define your fitness goals, such as improving cardiovascular health, building strength, or enhancing flexibility.
2. **Create a Balanced Routine**: Include a mix of cardio, strength training, and flexibility exercises in your routine.
3. **Schedule Regular Workouts**: Schedule your workouts at times that align with your energy levels and daily schedule.
4. **Monitor Progress**: Track your progress and adjust your routine as needed to ensure continuous improvement.

The Role of Nutrition in Energy Optimization

Nutrition provides the essential nutrients and fuel your body needs to maintain high energy levels and overall health.

- **Key Nutrients for Energy**
1. **Carbohydrates**: Carbohydrates are the body's primary source of energy. Choose complex carbohydrates such as whole grains, fruits, and vegetables for sustained energy.
2. **Proteins**: Proteins are essential for muscle repair and growth. Include lean proteins such as chicken, fish, beans, and legumes in your diet.
3. **Fats**: Healthy fats provide long-lasting energy and support brain function. Incorporate sources of healthy fats such as avocados, nuts, seeds, and olive oil.
4. **Vitamins and Minerals:** Vitamins and minerals play critical roles in energy production and overall health. Ensure a varied diet that includes fruits, vegetables, and whole foods to obtain essential nutrients.
- **Hydration**

Staying hydrated is crucial for maintaining energy levels and overall health.

Exercise: Hydration Habits

1. **Drink Regularly**: Drink water throughout the day, even if you don't feel thirsty.
2. **Monitor Urine Color**: Aim for light yellow urine, indicating proper hydration.
3. **Limit Caffeine and Alcohol**: Reduce consumption of caffeine and alcohol, which can dehydrate the body.
- **Balanced Diet for Energy**

A balanced diet that includes a variety of nutrient-dense foods can help sustain energy levels throughout the day.

Exercise: Planning Balanced Meals

1. **Meal Planning**: Plan balanced meals that include a mix of carbohydrates, proteins, and healthy fats.

2. **Portion Control**: Pay attention to portion sizes to avoid overeating and maintain energy balance.
3. **Regular Meals and Snacks**: Eat regular meals and healthy snacks to maintain steady energy levels.

Examples of Balanced Meals

1. **Breakfast**: Greek yogurt with berries, whole grain toast with avocado, and a boiled egg.
2. **Lunch**: Grilled chicken salad with mixed greens, quinoa, and a vinaigrette dressing.
3. **Dinner**: Baked salmon with roasted vegetables and brown rice.
4. **Snacks**: Apple slices with almond butter, carrot sticks with hummus, or a handful of nuts.
- **Nutrition Timing**

The timing of your meals can also impact your energy levels.

Exercise: Optimizing Nutrition Timing

1. **Breakfast**: Eat a nutritious breakfast to kickstart your metabolism and provide energy for the day.
2. **Pre-Workout**: Consume a light snack or meal with carbohydrates and protein 30-60 minutes before exercise.
3. **Post-Workout**: Eat a meal or snack with protein and carbohydrates within 30 minutes after exercise to support recovery.
4. **Regular Intervals**: Eat regular meals and snacks every 3-4 hours to maintain steady energy levels.
- **Supplements for Energy**

While a balanced diet is the best way to obtain essential nutrients, certain supplements can help support energy levels.

Exercise: Choosing Supplements

1. **Consult a Professional**: Consult with a healthcare professional before taking any supplements.
2. **Common Supplements**: Common supplements for energy include multivitamins, vitamin D, B vitamins, and omega-3 fatty acids.
3. **Quality and Dosage**: Choose high-quality supplements and follow recommended dosages to avoid potential side effects.

Mental and Emotional Health

Mental and emotional health is foundational to energy optimization. Your thoughts, emotions, and psychological well-being directly impact your energy levels, productivity, and overall quality of life. Mental health refers to your cognitive functioning, including how you process information, solve problems, and make decisions. Emotional health involves your ability to understand, manage, and express your emotions effectively. Both are interconnected and significantly influence your energy levels.

Addressing mental and emotional health involves managing stress, building resilience, and fostering positive mental habits.

The Impact of Mental and Emotional Health on Energy

1. **Stress and Energy Depletion**: Chronic stress drains your energy, impairs cognitive function, and can lead to physical health issues. Managing stress effectively is essential for maintaining high energy levels.
2. **Emotional Resilience**: Building emotional resilience helps you cope with challenges and bounce back from setbacks, preserving your energy and well-being.
3. **Positive Mental Habits**: Cultivating positive mental habits, such as gratitude and mindfulness, enhances emotional well-being and boosts energy levels.

Strategies for Optimizing Mental and Emotional Health

- **Stress Management Techniques**

Effective stress management is crucial for maintaining mental and emotional health. Here are some techniques to manage stress and optimize energy:

Exercise: Stress Management Techniques

1. **Deep Breathing**: Practice deep breathing exercises to calm your mind and reduce stress. Inhale deeply through your nose, hold for a few seconds, and exhale slowly through your mouth. Repeat several times.
2. **Progressive Muscle Relaxation**: Practice progressive muscle relaxation by tensing and then relaxing each muscle group in your body, starting from your toes and working up to your head.
3. **Visualization**: Use visualization techniques to imagine a peaceful and relaxing scene. Picture yourself in a calm environment, such as a beach or forest, and focus on the sensory details.
4. **Mindfulness Meditation**: Practice mindfulness meditation to stay present and reduce anxiety. Focus on your breath and observe your thoughts without judgment.
5. **Physical Activity**: Engage in regular physical activity, such as walking, jogging, or yoga, to release endorphins and reduce stress.

- **Building Emotional Resilience**

Emotional resilience is the ability to adapt to stress and adversity, maintaining emotional balance and energy. Here are some strategies to build emotional resilience:

Exercise: Building Emotional Resilience

1. **Cognitive Restructuring**: Practice cognitive restructuring to challenge and change negative thought patterns. Identify negative thoughts, evaluate their accuracy, and replace them with more positive and realistic ones.
2. **Emotional Awareness**: Develop emotional awareness by regularly checking in with your emotions. Recognize and label your feelings, and understand the triggers behind them.
3. **Self-Compassion**: Practice self-compassion by treating yourself with kindness and understanding during difficult times. Acknowledge your struggles without self-criticism.
4. **Social Support**: Build a strong support network of friends, family, and colleagues. Reach out for support when needed and offer support to others.
5. **Problem-Solving Skills**: Enhance your problem-solving skills by breaking down challenges into manageable steps. Develop and implement effective solutions.

- **Cultivating Positive Mental Habits**

Positive mental habits can enhance emotional well-being and boost energy levels. Here are some habits to cultivate:

Exercise: Cultivating Positive Mental Habits

1. **Gratitude Practice**: Develop a gratitude practice by regularly reflecting on and writing down things you are grateful for. This habit can improve mood and energy.
2. **Positive Affirmations**: Use positive affirmations to reinforce positive beliefs and attitudes. Repeat affirmations daily, such as "I am capable and confident" or "I handle challenges with grace."
3. **Mindful Living**: Incorporate mindfulness into your daily routine. Practice being fully present in each moment, whether you are eating, walking, or working.

4. **Journaling**: Keep a journal to express and process your thoughts and emotions. Reflect on positive experiences and achievements.
5. **Acts of Kindness**: Perform acts of kindness for others. Helping others can boost your mood and energy, creating a positive feedback loop.

Recharging Rituals

In our fast-paced world, it's easy to get caught up in the whirlwind of constant activity and forget the importance of taking breaks and engaging in restorative activities. Recharging rituals are essential practices that help rejuvenate your energy levels, maintain mental clarity, and enhance overall well-being. Recharging rituals refer to the intentional practices you incorporate into your daily routine to restore and maintain your energy levels. These rituals can range from short breaks and micro-breaks to more extended periods of rest and engaging in activities that rejuvenate your mind and body.

By incorporating regular breaks and restorative activities into your daily routine, you can optimize your productivity and ensure that you stay energized throughout the day.

The Importance of Recharging Rituals

1. **Enhanced Productivity**: Regular breaks help prevent burnout and maintain high levels of productivity throughout the day.
2. **Improved Focus**: Taking time to recharge allows you to return to tasks with renewed focus and concentration.
3. **Reduced Stress**: Engaging in restorative activities helps manage stress and promotes mental and emotional well-being.

4. **Better Health**: Recharging rituals support overall physical health by reducing the risk of fatigue and related health issues.

Components of Recharging Rituals

Recharging rituals can be divided into two main components:

1. **Breaks and Micro-Breaks**: Short, frequent breaks that allow you to rest and recharge briefly throughout the day.
2. **Restorative Activities**: Longer, more intentional activities that provide deeper relaxation and rejuvenation.

Breaks and Micro-Breaks

Breaks and micro-breaks are short periods of rest taken during work or other activities to prevent fatigue and maintain productivity. These breaks can range from a few seconds to several minutes and are designed to provide quick refreshment and prevent burnout.

Research has shown that taking regular breaks can significantly enhance cognitive function, reduce stress, and improve overall well-being. The brain is not designed to maintain prolonged periods of intense focus without rest. By incorporating breaks and micro-breaks, you allow your brain to recover, process information, and maintain optimal performance.

Types of Breaks and Micro-Breaks

1. **Micro-Breaks**: Very short breaks, usually lasting 30 seconds to 2 minutes, taken frequently throughout the day.
2. **Short Breaks**: Breaks lasting 5-15 minutes, typically taken every hour or after completing a task.
3. **Extended Breaks**: Longer breaks, lasting 30-60 minutes, taken during lunch or after several hours of work.

Benefits of Breaks and Micro-Breaks

1. **Increased Alertness**: Short breaks help maintain alertness and prevent the decline in cognitive performance associated with prolonged focus.
2. **Reduced Fatigue**: Regular breaks help reduce physical and mental fatigue, allowing you to sustain high energy levels.
3. **Improved Creativity**: Breaks provide an opportunity for your mind to wander and make new connections, enhancing creativity and problem-solving skills.
4. **Enhanced Mood**: Taking breaks helps reduce stress and improve mood, contributing to overall emotional well-being.

Strategies for Effective Breaks and Micro-Breaks

1. **Pomodoro Technique**: The Pomodoro Technique consists of working in focused intervals of 25 minutes, followed by a 5-minute break. After completing four intervals, you take a longer break of 15-30 minutes.
2. **90-Minute Work Cycles**: Based on ultradian rhythms, work for 90-minute cycles followed by a 15-20 minute break.
3. **Scheduled Breaks**: Set specific times for breaks throughout the day to ensure you take regular rest periods.

Exercise: Implementing Breaks and Micro-Breaks

1. **Plan Your Breaks**: Schedule breaks and micro-breaks into your daily routine. Use a timer or app to remind you to take breaks.
2. **Incorporate Movement**: Use breaks to stretch, walk, or engage in light physical activity to improve circulation and reduce muscle tension.

3. **Mental Refresh**: Use breaks to rest your mind by practicing deep breathing, meditation, or simply closing your eyes for a few moments.
4. **Hydration and Nutrition**: Use breaks to hydrate and have a healthy snack to maintain energy levels.

Examples of Effective Micro-Breaks

1. **Deep Breathing**: Take 1-2 minutes to practice deep breathing exercises. Inhale deeply through your nose, hold for a few seconds, and exhale slowly through your mouth.
2. **Stretching**: Perform a quick stretching routine to relieve muscle tension. Focus on stretching areas that feel tight, such as your neck, shoulders, and back.
3. **Mindful Observation**: Spend a minute observing your surroundings mindfully. Notice the colors, shapes, and details around you without judgment.
4. **Gratitude Practice**: Take a moment to think of something you are grateful for. This simple practice can boost your mood and reduce stress.

Examples of Effective Short Breaks

1. **Walk Outside**: Take a 5-10 minute walk outside to get fresh air and change your environment.
2. **Healthy Snack**: Have a healthy snack, such as a piece of fruit or a handful of nuts, to refuel your body.
3. **Social Interaction**: Engage in a brief conversation with a colleague or friend to take your mind off work and boost your mood.
4. **Meditation**: Practice a short guided meditation to clear your mind and reduce stress.

Examples of Effective Extended Breaks

1. **Lunch Break**: Use your lunch break to enjoy a nutritious meal and engage in a relaxing activity, such as reading or listening to music.
2. **Exercise Session**: Use an extended break to engage in a physical activity, such as a workout or yoga session, to boost energy levels and improve mood.
3. **Creative Activity**: Engage in a creative activity, such as drawing, painting, or playing a musical instrument, to stimulate your mind and relax.
4. **Nature Walk**: Take a walk in nature to benefit from the calming effects of the natural environment.

Restorative Activities

Restorative activities are intentional practices that provide deeper relaxation and rejuvenation. These activities go beyond short breaks and are designed to recharge your physical, mental, and emotional energy.

The Importance of Restorative Activities

Restorative activities are essential for:

1. **Deep Relaxation**: Providing a deeper level of relaxation that helps reset your mind and body.
2. **Stress Reduction**: Reducing stress and promoting emotional well-being.
3. **Enhanced Recovery**: Supporting recovery from physical and mental exertion, preventing burnout.
4. **Improved Overall Health**: Contributing to overall physical and mental health by promoting balance and well-being.

Types of Restorative Activities

Restorative activities can be categorized into physical, mental, and emotional practices. Incorporating a variety of these activities into your routine ensures comprehensive recharging.

Physical Restorative Activities

Exercise: Engaging in Physical Restorative Activities

1. **Yoga**: Practice yoga to improve flexibility, strength, and relaxation. Yoga combines physical postures with breathing exercises and meditation, providing a holistic approach to restoration.
2. **Massage**: Schedule regular massages to relieve muscle tension, improve circulation, and promote relaxation.
3. **Tai Chi**: Practice Tai Chi to enhance balance, flexibility, and mental clarity. This gentle martial art involves slow, flowing movements and deep breathing.
4. **Stretching Routine**: Develop a daily stretching routine to release muscle tension and improve flexibility.

Benefits of Physical Restorative Activities

1. **Improved Physical Health**: Physical restorative activities enhance overall physical health by reducing muscle tension, improving circulation, and promoting relaxation.
2. **Enhanced Flexibility**: Regular practice of activities like yoga and stretching improves flexibility and reduces the risk of injury.
3. **Reduced Stress**: Physical activities that incorporate mindful movement and breathing help reduce stress and promote a sense of calm.
- **Mental Restorative Activities**

Exercise: Engaging in Mental Restorative Activities

1. **Meditation**: Practice meditation to calm your mind and improve focus. Meditation involves focusing your attention and eliminating distractions, promoting mental clarity and relaxation.
2. **Mindfulness**: Incorporate mindfulness practices into your daily routine. Mindfulness involves paying attention to the present moment without judgment, helping reduce stress and enhance mental well-being.
3. **Reading**: Engage in reading for pleasure to stimulate your mind and provide mental escape. Choose books that interest and inspire you.
4. **Puzzles and Games**: Solve puzzles or play games that challenge your mind and provide mental stimulation. Activities like crossword puzzles, Sudoku, and board games can be enjoyable and restorative.

Benefits of Mental Restorative Activities

1. **Enhanced Cognitive Function**: Mental restorative activities stimulate the brain, improving cognitive function and mental clarity.
2. **Reduced Mental Fatigue**: Engaging in mentally stimulating activities helps reduce mental fatigue and refresh the mind.
3. **Improved Focus**: Practices like meditation and mindfulness enhance focus and concentration, leading to better productivity.
   - **Emotional Restorative Activities**

Exercise: Engaging in Emotional Restorative Activities

1. **Journaling**: Practice journaling to express and process emotions. Writing about your thoughts and feelings can provide emotional release and clarity.

2. **Art Therapy**: Engage in creative activities such as drawing, painting, or sculpting to express emotions and reduce stress. Art therapy provides a non-verbal outlet for emotional expression.
3. **Music Therapy**: Listen to or play music to enhance emotional well-being. Music has a powerful impact on emotions and can be used to relax, energize, or uplift your mood.
4. **Gratitude Practice**: Develop a gratitude practice by regularly reflecting on and writing down things you are grateful for. This practice can boost mood and promote emotional resilience.

Benefits of Emotional Restorative Activities

1. **Emotional Release**: Emotional restorative activities provide an outlet for expressing and processing emotions, reducing emotional tension.
2. **Improved Mood**: Engaging in activities that promote emotional well-being can improve mood and reduce stress.
3. **Enhanced Resilience**: Regular practice of emotional restorative activities builds emotional resilience, helping you cope with challenges more effectively.

Combining Breaks and Restorative Activities

Combining breaks and restorative activities into a cohesive routine can maximize their benefits and ensure you stay energized and focused throughout the day.

Exercise: Creating a Recharging Routine

1. **Plan Your Day**: Plan your day to include regular breaks and restorative activities. Use a planner or calendar to schedule these activities.

2. **Mix and Match**: Combine different types of breaks and restorative activities to address your physical, mental, and emotional needs. For example, start your day with a stretching routine, take micro-breaks for deep breathing, and engage in a creative activity during your lunch break.
3. **Adjust as Needed**: Adjust your routine based on your needs and preferences. Experiment with different activities and schedules to find what works best for you.
4. **Reflect on Benefits**: Regularly reflect on the benefits of your recharging routine. Notice how these practices impact your energy levels, focus, and overall well-being.

Remember that recharging rituals are highly individual, and it's important to find practices that work best for you. Experiment with different types of breaks and restorative activities, and adjust your routine based on your needs and preferences. With a well-balanced recharging routine, you can stay energized, focused, and resilient in both your professional and personal life. Embrace the power of recharging rituals and make them an integral part of your daily routine to achieve sustained productivity and overall well-being.

Key Takeaways

1. Energy management optimizes your physical, emotional, and mental energy to maintain high productivity and avoid burnout.
2. Understanding your natural energy cycles, such as ultradian rhythms, helps align tasks with peak performance periods.
3. Regular breaks and restorative activities are crucial for maintaining energy levels and preventing fatigue.
4. A balanced diet, regular exercise, and quality sleep are fundamental to sustaining physical energy.
5. Mental and emotional well-being, including stress management and positive habits, significantly impact your overall energy.

Reflective Questions

1. What are your peak energy periods during the day, and how can you align your most demanding tasks with these times?
2. How do you currently manage breaks and restorative activities throughout your day, and what changes could improve your energy levels?
3. In what ways can you optimize your diet, exercise, and sleep to enhance your physical energy?
4. What strategies can you implement to better manage stress and support your emotional energy?
5. How can you incorporate mindfulness and positive mental habits into your daily routine to boost your overall energy and well-being?

CHAPTER 7
Creating Focus-Friendly Habits

Building focus-friendly habits is a fundamental aspect of optimizing your productivity and achieving long-term goals. Habits are the routines and behaviors that we perform almost automatically, often without conscious thought. These habits can either support our focus and productivity or hinder them. By understanding the mechanics of habit formation and leveraging this knowledge, we can design and sustain habits that enhance our ability to concentrate and work effectively.

In this chapter, we will explore the power of habits, the habit loop, and the habit formation process. We will delve into how habits are formed, the psychology behind them, and practical strategies to build and sustain habits that promote focus and productivity.

Introduction to Creating Focus-Friendly Habits

Habits are powerful because they shape our daily actions and, ultimately, our lives. Creating focus-friendly habits involves identifying behaviors that support sustained concentration and integrating them into your routine. This process requires understanding how habits work, how they are formed, and how they can be modified to suit your goals.

Why Habits Matter for Focus

1. **Automaticity**: Habits allow behaviors to become automatic, reducing the cognitive load required to perform them. This frees up mental resources for more demanding tasks.

2. **Consistency**: Well-established habits create consistency and routine, which are essential for maintaining focus over time.
3. **Efficiency**: Habits streamline daily actions, making processes more efficient and less mentally taxing.
4. **Stress Reduction**: Having positive habits in place reduces the need for constant decision-making, lowering stress levels and promoting mental clarity.

The Power of Habits

Habits are behaviors that are repeated regularly and tend to occur subconsciously. They are formed through a process in which a behavior becomes automatic after repeated exposure to a specific cue or context. The power of habits lies in their ability to influence our actions and decisions, often without us even realizing it.

The Habit Loop

The habit loop is a simple framework that explains how habits are formed and maintained. It consists of three main components: the cue, the routine, and the reward. Understanding this loop is crucial for creating and sustaining focus-friendly habits.

- **Cue**

The cue is the trigger that initiates the habit. It can be a specific time of day, an emotional state, a particular location, or any other context that signals the start of the behavior.

Examples of Cues:
- A specific time, such as waking up or returning from lunch.
- An emotional state, such as feeling stressed or bored.
- A location, such as your desk or a particular room.
- A preceding action, such as finishing a meeting or completing a task.

Exercise: Identifying Cues

1. **Observe Triggers**: Over the course of a week, observe the triggers that lead to specific behaviors. Note the context, time, location, and emotional state associated with each behavior.
2. **Record Patterns**: Record these observations in a journal to identify patterns and common cues that trigger your habits.
3. **Analyze Data**: Analyze the data to understand which cues are most influential in initiating your habits.

- **Routine**

The routine is the behavior or action that follows the cue. This is the habit itself, which can be positive, such as exercising or meditating, or negative, such as procrastinating or snacking on unhealthy foods.

Examples of Routines:

- Going for a run in the morning.
- Checking emails immediately after sitting down at your desk.
- Meditating before bed.
- Snacking while watching TV.

Exercise: Evaluating Routines

1. **List Routines**: Make a list of your daily routines and categorize them as positive, negative, or neutral.
2. **Assess Impact**: Assess the impact of each routine on your focus and productivity. Identify which routines support your goals and which ones hinder them.
3. **Prioritize Changes**: Prioritize the routines that you want to change or reinforce based on their impact.

- **Reward**

The reward is the positive reinforcement that follows the routine, which makes the behavior satisfying and encourages its repetition.

Rewards can be intrinsic, such as a sense of accomplishment, or extrinsic, such as a treat or praise.

Examples of Rewards:
- Feeling energized after a workout.
- Experiencing a sense of relief after checking off a to-do list item.
- Enjoying a piece of chocolate after completing a task.
- Receiving praise for a job well done.

Exercise: Identifying Rewards
1. **Identify Rewards**: Identify the rewards associated with your routines. Note how each reward makes you feel and why it reinforces the behavior.
2. **Evaluate Satisfaction**: Evaluate the satisfaction level of each reward. Determine if the reward is meaningful and motivating enough to sustain the habit.
3. **Enhance Rewards**: Consider ways to enhance or modify rewards to make them more effective in reinforcing positive habits.

Habit Formation Process

The habit formation process involves several stages, from initial adoption to automaticity. Understanding these stages can help you develop and sustain habits that support your focus and productivity.

Stages of Habit Formation
- **Initiation**

The initiation stage involves deciding to adopt a new habit and taking the first steps toward implementing it. This stage requires motivation and commitment.

Strategies for Initiation:

1. **Set Clear Goals**: Define clear, specific goals for the habit you want to adopt. For example, "I will meditate for 10 minutes every morning."
2. **Start Small**: Begin with manageable steps to build momentum. For example, start with 5 minutes of meditation and gradually increase the duration.
3. **Create a Plan**: Develop a detailed plan for how and when you will perform the habit. Consider potential obstacles and how you will overcome them.

Exercise: Initiating a New Habit

1. **Define Your Habit**: Clearly define the habit you want to adopt and why it is important to you.
2. **Set a Start Date**: Choose a specific date to begin implementing the habit.
3. **Prepare in Advance**: Gather any necessary materials or resources and create a plan for incorporating the habit into your routine.

- **Formation**

The formation stage involves repeating the behavior consistently until it becomes more familiar and easier to perform. This stage requires discipline and persistence.

Strategies for Formation

1. **Consistency**: Perform the habit at the same time and in the same context each day to strengthen the association between the cue and the routine.
2. **Tracking Progress**: Keep a habit tracker or journal to monitor your progress and stay motivated.
3. **Seek Support**: Share your goals with a friend or join a community with similar interests to gain support and accountability.

Exercise: Forming a New Habit

1. **Create a Habit Tracker**: Use a habit tracker to record each instance of performing the habit. Mark off each day you complete the habit.
2. **Reflect on Challenges**: Reflect on any challenges or obstacles you encounter and develop strategies to overcome them.
3. **Celebrate Milestones**: Celebrate small milestones and successes to maintain motivation and reinforce the habit.

- **Maintenance**

The maintenance stage involves continuing the behavior over a longer period until it becomes automatic. This stage requires resilience and adaptability.

Strategies for Maintenance:

1. **Adjust as Needed**: Adjust your approach if you encounter obstacles or if your circumstances change. Flexibility is key to maintaining the habit.
2. **Reinforce Rewards**: Ensure that the rewards associated with the habit remain meaningful and motivating.
3. **Review and Reflect**: Regularly review your progress and reflect on the benefits of the habit to reinforce its importance.

Exercise: Maintaining a New Habit

1. **Regular Reflection**: Reflect on your progress at regular intervals, such as weekly or monthly. Note any improvements in focus, productivity, or well-being.
2. **Adapt to Changes**: Be prepared to adapt your habits to accommodate changes in your schedule or environment.
3. **Stay Committed**: Stay committed to the habit, even if progress is slow or setbacks occur. Persistence is key to long-term success.

- **Automaticity**

The automaticity stage is when the behavior becomes ingrained and requires little conscious effort to perform. The habit is now a natural part of your routine.

Strategies for Achieving Automaticity:

1. **Repetition**: Continue to perform the habit consistently until it becomes second nature.
2. **Strengthen** Associations: Reinforce the association between the cue and the routine to ensure the habit is triggered automatically.
3. **Monitor for Maintenance**: Occasionally review the habit to make sure it remains effective and aligned with your goals.

Exercise: Achieving Automaticity

1. **Consistent Practice**: Continue practicing the habit consistently, even after it becomes easier and more automatic.
2. **Strengthen the Cue**: Reinforce the cue to ensure it reliably triggers the routine. For example, if the cue is an alarm, ensure it is set at the same time each day.
3. **Periodic Reflection**: Regularly evaluate the habit to ensure it stays aligned with your goals and continues to offer benefits.

Designing Productive Habits

Designing productive habits involves intentionally creating routines that support your goals and enhance your focus. This process requires understanding your personal preferences, motivations, and the specific behaviors that will help you achieve your objectives.

Identifying Productive Habits

1. **Goal Alignment**: Identify habits that align with your long-term goals. For example, if your goal is to improve your focus at work, consider habits like time blocking, regular breaks, and mindfulness practice.
2. **Personal Preferences**: Take into account your personal preferences and what suits you best. Some people may find morning exercise beneficial, while others may prefer evening workouts.
3. **Behavioral Specificity**: Be specific about the behaviors you want to incorporate. Instead of a vague goal like "exercise more," be specific with "run for 20 minutes every morning."

Exercise: Identifying Productive Habits

1. **Define Goals**: Document your long-term goals and pinpoint the habits that will help you achieve them.
2. **Personal Preferences**: Reflect on your preferences and daily schedule. Choose habits that fit naturally into your routine.
3. **Specify Behaviors**: Clearly define the specific behaviors you want to adopt. Ensure they are actionable and measurable.

Creating a Plan for Productive Habits

1. **SMART Goals**: Use the SMART criteria (Specific, Measurable, Achievable, Relevant, Time-bound) to set clear goals for your habits.
2. **Action Steps**: Break down the habit into smaller, manageable action steps. For example, if your habit is to meditate daily, start with 5 minutes and gradually increase the duration.

3. **Cue Integration**: Integrate cues into your daily routine to trigger the habit. For example, place your meditation cushion where you can see it as a reminder to meditate.

Exercise: Creating a Plan

1. **Set SMART Goals**: Define SMART goals for your habits. For example, "I will meditate for 10 minutes every morning for the next month."
2. **Break Down Steps**: Outline the action steps needed to achieve the habit. For meditation, this might include finding a quiet space, setting a timer, and choosing a guided meditation app.
3. **Identify Cues**: Identify and integrate cues into your routine. Place visual reminders or set alarms to trigger the habit.

Implementing and Adjusting Habits

1. **Start Small**: Begin with small, achievable steps to build momentum. Gradually increase the difficulty or duration of the habit.
2. **Monitor Progress**: Regularly monitor your progress and make adjustments as needed. Use a habit tracker or journal to stay accountable.
3. **Adapt to Changes**: Be adaptable and adjust your habits to fit changes in your schedule or environment. Continuously refine your approach to ensure the habit remains effective.

Exercise: Implementing and Adjusting Habits

1. **Start with Small Steps**: Begin with small, manageable steps to build confidence and momentum.
2. **Track Progress**: Utilize a habit tracker or journal to monitor your progress and reflect on your experiences.

3. **Make Adjustments**: Adjust your habits as needed based on your progress and any challenges you encounter. Stay flexible and open to changes.

Sustaining Habits Long-Term

Sustaining habits long-term requires ongoing commitment, adaptability, and reinforcement. It's essential to develop strategies that help you maintain your habits over time and overcome challenges that may arise.

Strategies for Sustaining Habits
- **Consistency and Routine**

Consistency is key to sustaining habits long-term. Establishing a routine helps reinforce the habit and makes it easier to maintain.

Exercise: Maintaining Consistency
1. **Daily Routine**: Incorporate the habit into your daily routine at the same time each day. Consistency helps reinforce the behavior.
2. **Visual Reminders**: Use visual reminders, such as sticky notes or alarms, to prompt you to perform the habit.
3. **Accountability Partner**: Find an accountability partner to share your goals with and check in regularly. Support from others can help you stay on track.
- **Overcoming Plateaus**

It's common to encounter plateaus where progress slows or the habit becomes challenging to maintain. Overcoming these plateaus is essential for long-term success.

Exercise: Overcoming Plateaus

1. **Reflect and Adjust**: Reflect on your progress and identify any obstacles or challenges. Adjust your approach as needed to overcome these barriers.
2. **Change the Routine**: Introduce variety into your routine to keep the habit engaging. For example, if you're bored with your exercise routine, try a new activity or workout.
3. **Set New Goals**: Set new, incremental goals to challenge yourself and maintain motivation. For example, increase your daily word count goal or try a new writing prompt.

Reinforcing Rewards

Rewards play a crucial role in sustaining habits. Ensuring that the rewards remain meaningful and motivating is essential for long-term maintenance.

Exercise: Reinforcing Rewards

1. **Identify Meaningful Rewards**: Identify rewards that are meaningful and motivating to you. These can be intrinsic rewards, such as a sense of accomplishment, or extrinsic rewards, such as a treat or leisure activity.
2. **Regular Reflection**: Regularly reflect on the benefits and rewards of the habit. Acknowledge the positive impact it has on your focus and productivity.
3. **Celebrate Milestones**: Celebrate milestones and successes to reinforce the habit. Recognize and reward yourself for achieving specific goals or maintaining consistency.
   - **Adapting to Changes**

Life is dynamic, and circumstances change. Adapting your habits to accommodate these changes is essential for sustaining them long-term.

Exercise: Adapting Habits

1. **Flexibility**: Be flexible and open to adjusting your habits as needed. If your schedule changes, find new times or contexts to perform the habit.
2. **Continuous Improvement**: Continuously seek ways to improve and optimize your habits. Reflect on what works and what doesn't, and make adjustments accordingly.
3. **Long-Term Vision**: Keep your long-term goals in view and concentrate on the bigger picture. Remember why the habit matters and how it contributes to your overall well-being and success.

Creating focus-friendly habits involves understanding the power of habits, the habit loop, and the habit formation process. By identifying productive habits, designing a clear plan, and implementing strategies to sustain them long-term, you can optimize your focus, productivity, and overall well-being.

Habit formation is a continuous process that demands commitment, adaptability, and reinforcement. Embrace the power of habits and make intentional choices to build routines that support your goals and enhance your life. With dedication and persistence, you can create and sustain habits that lead to long-term success and fulfillment.

Key Takeaways

1. Habits can significantly influence focus and productivity by reducing the cognitive load required for routine tasks.
2. The habit loop, consisting of cue, routine, and reward, is fundamental to understanding and shaping habits.
3. Consistency and repetition are crucial for habit formation, transforming intentional actions into automatic behaviors.

4. Identifying and integrating productive habits aligned with personal goals and preferences can enhance focus and efficiency.
5. Sustaining habits long-term requires adaptability, reinforcement of rewards, and overcoming plateaus.

Reflective Questions

1. What cues can you identify in your daily routine that trigger your current habits, and how can you leverage them to develop focus-friendly habits?
2. Which current habits are negatively impacting your focus and productivity, and how can you modify or replace them with more positive routines?
3. How can you design a plan to integrate new habits that support your long-term goals, and what specific action steps will you take?
4. What rewards can you use to reinforce your new habits, ensuring they remain meaningful and motivating over time?
5. How will you adapt your habits to accommodate changes in your schedule or environment, maintaining consistency and progress?

CONCLUSION

As we conclude this book, it's time to pause and reflect on the journey we've taken together. This book has been a companion, a guide, and a resource, helping you navigate the complexities of maintaining focus in an increasingly distracting world. Now, as you stand on the cusp of implementing these strategies into your daily life, it's important to remember the essence of focus and the power it holds.

Focus is not just about eliminating distractions or managing your time more efficiently; it's about connecting deeply with your goals, values, and aspirations. It's about recognizing what truly matters to you and dedicating your energy and attention to those pursuits. When you focus, you're not just working - you're creating, growing, and becoming the best version of yourself.

In your journey ahead, challenges will inevitably arise. There will be days when distractions seem insurmountable, when your motivation wanes, and when you experience son setbacks. But it's in these moments that your commitment to focus will truly be tested and strengthened. Embrace these challenges as opportunities to practice resilience and determination. Remember, each small step you take towards improving your focus is a victory in itself.

The strategies and techniques discussed in this book are tools in your toolkit. They are meant to be adapted and molded to fit your unique life and circumstances. Be flexible and patient with yourself. Progress may sometimes be slow, but it is progress nonetheless. Celebrate your small wins and use them as fuel to keep moving forward.

As you implement these practices, don't forget the importance of balance. Focus should not come at the expense of your well-being. Take time to rest, recharge, and engage in activities that bring you joy and fulfillment. A well-rounded approach to life will ensure that your focus is sustainable and enriching.

You have the power to shape your destiny through the choices you make each day. By prioritizing focus, you're investing in your future success and happiness. Imagine the satisfaction of looking back and seeing the tangible results of your dedicated efforts—the projects completed, the goals achieved, and the personal growth realized.

Let this be your reminder that focus is not a destination. It's a continuous process of aligning your actions with your intentions, of striving for excellence while being kind to yourself. It's about building a life that reflects your true potential and aspirations.

So, as you close this book, take a deep breath and recommit to your journey of focus. You have the knowledge, the tools, and the inner strength to make meaningful progress. Trust in yourself and the process. Stay curious, stay motivated, and above all, stay focused.

Cheers to your success, to your growth, and to the incredible journey that lies ahead. May you discover your true potential and craft a life filled with purpose, passion, and steadfast focus.

Thank you for allowing this book to be a part of your journey. The best is yet to come.

Printed in Great Britain
by Amazon